ENGLISH
FOR EVERYONE

ENGLISH PHRASAL VERBS

FREE AUDIO
website and app
www.dkefe.com

Authors

Thomas Booth worked for 10 years as an English-language teacher in Poland and Russia. He now lives in England, where he works as an editor and English-language materials writer. He has contributed to a number of books in the *English for Everyone* series.

Ben Ffrancon Davies is a freelance writer and translator. He writes textbooks and study guides on a wide range of subjects including ELT, music, and literature. Ben studied Medieval and Modern Languages at the University of Oxford, and has taught English in France and Spain.

UK language consultant

Peter Dainty studied History at the University of Oxford and has been teaching English as a foreign language since the mid-1980s. He taught at London University for 10 years and has written 14 books for publishers such as Macmillan, Penguin, Scholastic, and Oxford University Press.

US language consultant

Professor Emerita Susan Barduhn has contributed to numerous publications. She has also been President of IATEFL; Director of The Language Center, Nairobi; Deputy Director of International House, London; professor and Chair of the MATESOL program at SIT Graduate Institute. She is currently a freelance educational consultant for the US Department of State, the British Council, TransformELT, The Consultants-e, and Fulbright.

ENGLISH FOR EVERYONE

ENGLISH PHRASAL VERBS

DK

DK | Penguin Random House

US Editors Kayla Dugger, Lori Hand
Senior Editor Ben Ffrancon Davies
Senior Art Editors Clare Shedden, Amy Child
Illustrator Gus Scott
Managing Editor Christine Stroyan
Managing Art Editor Anna Hall
Production Editor George Nimmo
Production Controller Samantha Cross
Jacket Designer Surabhi Wadhwa-Gandhi
Jacket Design Development Manager Sophia MTT
Publisher Andrew Macintyre
Art Director Karen Self
Publishing Director Jonathan Metcalf

DK DELHI

Senior Editor Janashree Singha
Editors Nandini D. Tripathy, Rishi Bryan
Senior Art Editor Vikas Sachdeva
Project Art Editor Sourabh Challariya
Senior DTP Designer Tarun Sharma
DTP Designers Manish Upreti, Anita Yadav
Senior Jacket Designer Suhita Dharamjit
Senior Managing Art Editor Arunesh Talapatra
Managing Editor Soma B. Chowdhury
Pre-production Managers Balwant Singh, Sunil Sharma
Editorial Head Glenda Fernandes
Design Head Malavika Talukder

First American Edition, 2021
Published in the United States by DK Publishing,
a division of Penguin Random House LLC
1745 Broadway, 20th Floor, New York, NY 10019

25 10 9 8 7 6 5 4 3
003-334973-Feb/2023

Published in Great Britain by Dorling Kindersley Limited

A catalog record for this book is available from the Library of Congress.
Box set ISBN 978-0-7440-8186-2
ISBN 978-0-7440-2744-0

Printed and bound in China

www.dk.com

FSC www.fsc.org MIX Paper | Supporting responsible forestry FSC™ C018179

This book was made with Forest Stewardship Council™ certified paper – one small step in DK's commitment to a sustainable future.
Learn more at www.dk.com/uk/information/sustainability

Contents

How to use this book

English for Everyone: English Phrasal Verbs will help you learn, understand, and remember the most common phrasal verbs in English. Each of the 56 units in the book consists of a teaching spread on a subject or theme, with illustrated sentences to place the phrasal verbs in context, and then a practice spread with exercises to reinforce what you have learned. Listen to the free audio and repeat each phrasal verb and sentence. The answers to all the exercises are at the back of the book, along with a comprehensive index.

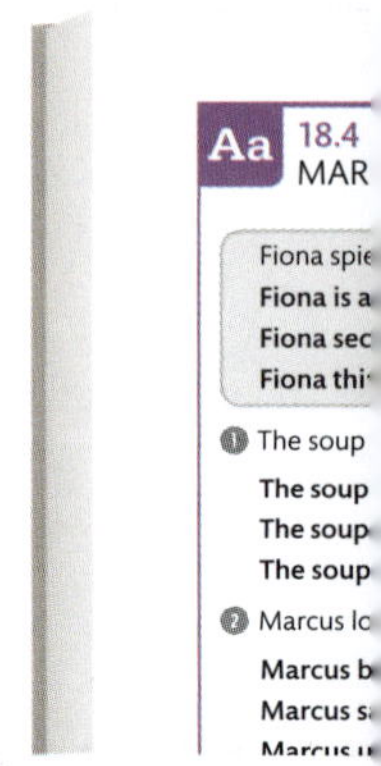

Unit number The book is divided into units. The unit number helps you keep track of your progress.

Sample sentences Phrasal verbs are shown in the context of a sample sentence (see page 8).

Module number Every module is identified with a unique number, so you can easily locate the related audio.

UK/US phrasal verbs Some phrasal verbs are specific to UK or US English. These are labeled (UK) or (US).

Base forms and definitions Beneath each sentence, the phrasal verb is written in its base form along with a definition.

Write-on lines You are encouraged to write your own translations of English phrasal verbs to create your own reference pages.

Modules Many teaching spreads are broken into modules covering different topics within the theme.

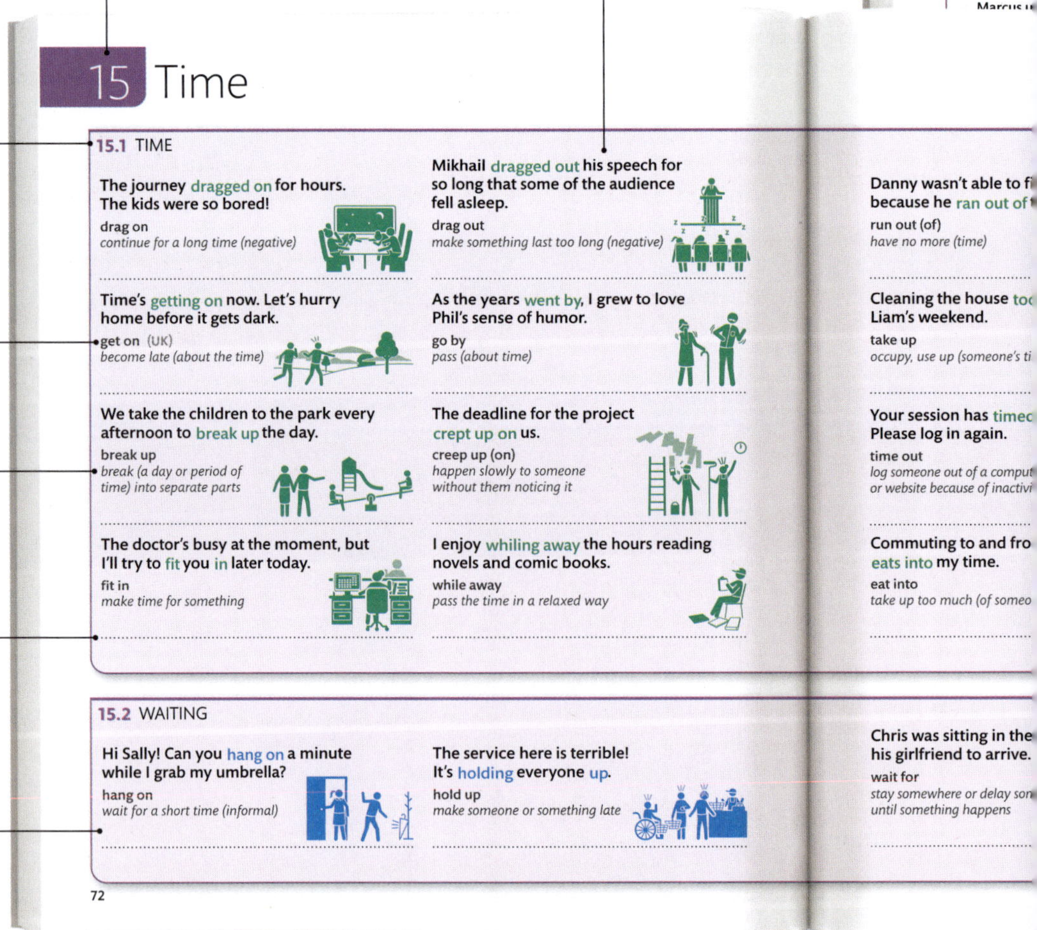
15 Time

15.1 TIME

The journey dragged on for hours. The kids were so bored!
drag on
continue for a long time (negative)

Mikhail dragged out his speech for so long that some of the audience fell asleep.
drag out
make something last too long (negative)

Danny wasn't able to fi
because he ran out of
run out (of)
have no more (time)

Time's getting on now. Let's hurry home before it gets dark.
get on (UK)
become late (about the time)

As the years went by, I grew to love Phil's sense of humor.
go by
pass (about time)

Cleaning the house too
Liam's weekend.
take up
occupy, use up (someone's ti

We take the children to the park every afternoon to break up the day.
break up
break (a day or period of time) into separate parts

The deadline for the project crept up on us.
creep up (on)
happen slowly to someone without them noticing it

Your session has timed
Please log in again.
time out
log someone out of a comput
or website because of inactivi

The doctor's busy at the moment, but I'll try to fit you in later today.
fit in
make time for something

I enjoy whiling away the hours reading novels and comic books.
while away
pass the time in a relaxed way

Commuting to and fro
eats into my time.
eat into
take up too much (of someo

15.2 WAITING

Hi Sally! Can you hang on a minute while I grab my umbrella?
hang on
wait for a short time (informal)

The service here is terrible! It's holding everyone up.
hold up
make someone or something late

Chris was sitting in the
his girlfriend to arrive.
wait for
stay somewhere or delay son
until something happens

72

TEACHING SPREAD

Listening exercise This symbol indicates that you should listen to an audio track in order to answer the questions in the exercise.

Exercise number Each exercise is identified with a unique number, so you can easily locate answers.

Sample answer The first question of each exercise is answered for you, to help make the task easy to understand.

Exercise instruction Each exercise is introduced with a brief instruction, telling you what you need to do.

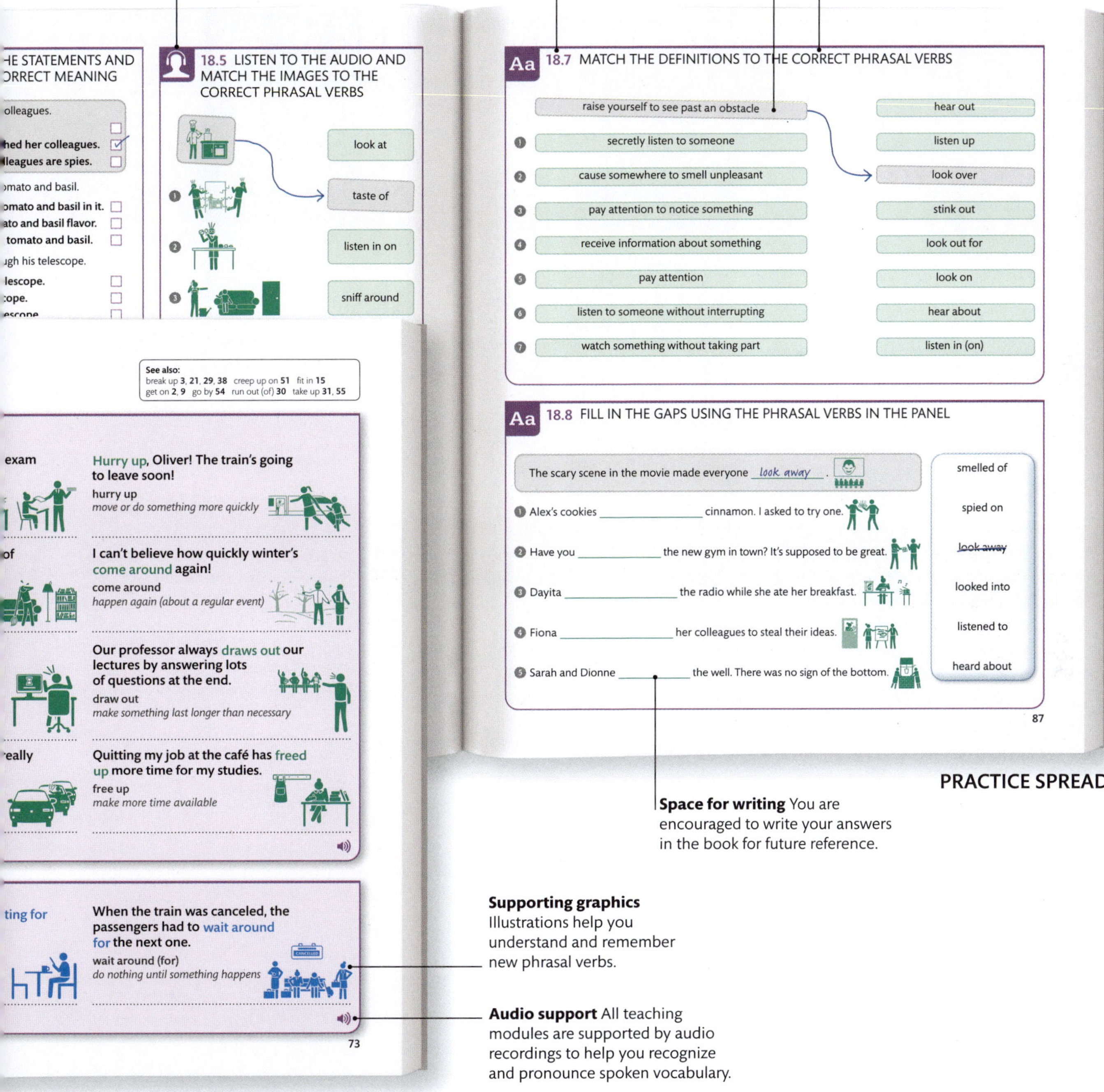

HE STATEMENTS AND
ORRECT MEANING

olleagues.
hed her colleagues.
lleagues are spies.
omato and basil.
omato and basil in it.
ato and basil flavor.
tomato and basil.
igh his telescope.
lescope.
cope.

18.5 LISTEN TO THE AUDIO AND MATCH THE IMAGES TO THE CORRECT PHRASAL VERBS

look at
taste of
listen in on
sniff around

See also:
break up 3, 21, 29, 38 creep up on 51 fit in 15
get on 2, 9 go by 54 run out (of) 30 take up 31, 55

exam

Hurry up, Oliver! The train's going to leave soon!
hurry up
move or do something more quickly

of

I can't believe how quickly winter's come around again!
come around
happen again (about a regular event)

Our professor always draws out our lectures by answering lots of questions at the end.
draw out
make something last longer than necessary

eally

Quitting my job at the café has freed up more time for my studies.
free up
make more time available

ting for

When the train was canceled, the passengers had to wait around for the next one.
wait around (for)
do nothing until something happens

73

18.7 MATCH THE DEFINITIONS TO THE CORRECT PHRASAL VERBS

raise yourself to see past an obstacle	hear out
1 secretly listen to someone	listen up
2 cause somewhere to smell unpleasant	look over
3 pay attention to notice something	stink out
4 receive information about something	look out for
5 pay attention	look on
6 listen to someone without interrupting	hear about
7 watch something without taking part	listen in (on)

18.8 FILL IN THE GAPS USING THE PHRASAL VERBS IN THE PANEL

The scary scene in the movie made everyone *look away*.

1 Alex's cookies ______ cinnamon. I asked to try one.

2 Have you ______ the new gym in town? It's supposed to be great.

3 Dayita ______ the radio while she ate her breakfast.

4 Fiona ______ her colleagues to steal their ideas.

5 Sarah and Dionne ______ the well. There was no sign of the bottom.

smelled of
spied on
~~look away~~
looked into
listened to
heard about

87

PRACTICE SPREAD

Space for writing You are encouraged to write your answers in the book for future reference.

Supporting graphics Illustrations help you understand and remember new phrasal verbs.

Audio support All teaching modules are supported by audio recordings to help you recognize and pronounce spoken vocabulary.

Sample sentences

Each phrasal verb is shown within a sample sentence that contextualizes its meaning. Its base form and definition are also given.

Phrasal verb The phrasal verb is highlighted in each sentence.

Illustration Each sentence is illustrated to show the meaning of the phrasal verb.

Angela meets up with her colleagues once a week to discuss all their new ideas.

Base form The phrasal verb is given in the base form.

meet up (with)

Definition A definition is given to help you understand the meaning.

get together with

Third particle Sometimes a phrasal verb's third particle is optional (see page 12), so it is written in parentheses.

"See also" boxes

Many phrasal verbs have more than one meaning. Each unit has a "see also" box which directs you to other units where the same phrasal verbs appear with different meanings.

Unit number This number tells you which other unit the phrasal verb appears in.

See also:
back up **12** climb down **19** fall out **49**
make up **41**, **52** take back **10**, **16**, **55**

DING CONFLICT

leagues always make fun
s, but he just laughs it off.

ticism or a difficult
uahing at it

Introducing phrasal verbs

Pages 10–17 contain an introductory grammar section explaining what phrasal verbs are and how they work grammatically. It also covers different types of phrasal verbs, as well as phrasal nouns and adjectives.

Modular learning The grammar section is broken down into modules.

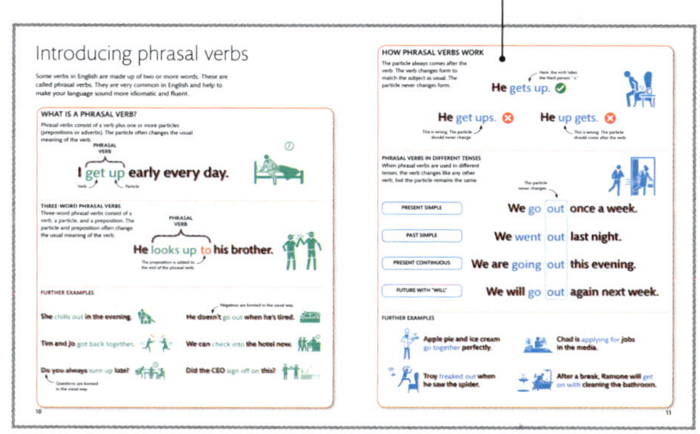

Audio

English for Everyone: English Phrasal Verbs offers extensive supporting audio resources. Every phrasal verb and sentence in the teaching spreads is recorded, and you are encouraged to listen to the audio and repeat the phrases and sentences out loud, until you are confident you understand and can pronounce what has been said.

SUPPORTING AUDIO
This symbol indicates that audio recordings of the phrasal verbs and sentences in a module are available for you to listen to.

LISTENING EXERCISES
This symbol indicates that you should listen to an audio track in order to answer the questions in the exercise.

FREE AUDIO
website and app
www.dkefe.com

Reference section

At the end of the book, pages 230–237 contain a reference section, which features additional information about phrasal verbs, including examples of some common phrasal nouns and phrasal adjectives.

Visual diagrams are used to present common particles.

Reference tables contain lists of common phrasal verbs, nouns, and adjectives.

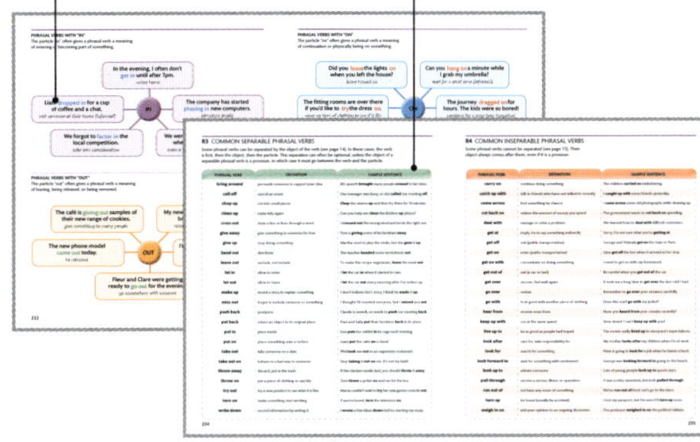

Answers

The book is designed to make it easy to monitor your progress. Answers are provided for every exercise, so you can see how well you have understood and remembered the phrasal verbs you have learned.

Answers Find the answers to every exercise printed at the back of the book.

Exercise numbers These numbers match the number at the top-left corner of each exercise.

25

25.3
1 The number of peo
online shot up last yea
2 The coach divided t
two equal teams.
3 Shreya counted up
wanting coffee and we
4 When Georgia was
she added on a 20% tip

25.4
A 3 B 1 C 6 D 2

25.5
1 Katie's bills have be
a lot of debt now.
2 The company's shar
but it's finally starting t
3 The temperature va
but it **averages out** at a
4 We estimated the c
to be £14,900, but **rou**
nearest thousand

Index

The index contains every phrasal verb from the teaching spreads, as well as the phrasal nouns and adjectives from the reference section, listed in alphabetical order, followed by each unit and module number where they appear.

M

Module number The number in the index matches the module number on the teaching page.

Multiple units When a phrasal verb appears more than once, each module number is listed.

Introducing phrasal verbs

Some verbs in English are made up of two or more words. These are called phrasal verbs. They are very common in English and help to make your language sound more idiomatic and fluent.

WHAT IS A PHRASAL VERB?

Phrasal verbs consist of a verb plus one or more particles (prepositions or adverbs). The particle often changes the usual meaning of the verb.

PHRASAL VERB

I get up early every day.

Verb: get — Particle: up

THREE-WORD PHRASAL VERBS

Three-word phrasal verbs consist of a verb, a particle, and a preposition. The particle and preposition often change the usual meaning of the verb.

PHRASAL VERB

He looks up to his brother.

The preposition is added to the end of the phrasal verb.

FURTHER EXAMPLES

She chills out in the evening.

Negatives are formed in the usual way.

He doesn't go out when he's tired.

Tim and Jo got back together.

We can check into the hotel now.

Do you always turn up late?

Questions are formed in the usual way.

Did the CEO sign off on this?

HOW PHRASAL VERBS WORK

The particle always comes after the verb. The verb changes form to match the subject as usual. The particle never changes form.

Here, the verb takes the third person "-s."

He gets up. ✓

He get ups. ✗

This is wrong. The particle should never change.

He up gets. ✗

This is wrong. The particle should come after the verb.

PHRASAL VERBS IN DIFFERENT TENSES

When phrasal verbs are used in different tenses, the verb changes like any other verb, but the particle remains the same.

The particle never changes.

PRESENT SIMPLE	We go out once a week.
PAST SIMPLE	We went out last night.
PRESENT CONTINUOUS	We are going out this evening.
FUTURE WITH "WILL"	We will go out again next week.

FURTHER EXAMPLES

Apple pie and ice cream go together perfectly.

Chad is applying for jobs in the media.

Troy freaked out when he saw the spider.

After a break, Ramone will get on with cleaning the bathroom.

TRANSITIVE AND INTRANSITIVE PHRASAL VERBS

Some phrasal verbs take an object, which is a noun that receives the action of the verb. Verbs which take an object are known as **transitive verbs**.

SUBJECT	PHRASAL VERB	OBJECT
Juan	measured out	the ingredients.

Some phrasal verbs do not take an object. These verbs are known as **intransitive verbs**.

SUBJECT	PHRASAL VERB
Tom	woke up.

Some phrasal verbs can be either **transitive or intransitive**.

SUBJECT	PHRASAL VERB	OBJECT
Idris	tidied up	the mess.

"Tidy up" can be used with or without an object.

MAKING INTRANSITIVE PHRASAL VERBS TRANSITIVE

Some intransitive phrasal verbs need a preposition when they are made transitive.

At the end of their stay, Julia and John checked out.

At the end of their stay, Julia and John checked out of their hotel.

To use "check out" with an object, you need to add "of."

FURTHER EXAMPLES

Julian usually heads off early to avoid the traffic.

Julian usually heads off to work early to avoid the traffic.

Ben and Gus finally made up after their argument.

Ben made up with Gus after their argument.

DIFFERENT MEANINGS

Many phrasal verbs have more than one meaning. Some phrasal verbs appear in this book more than once with a different meaning each time.

UNRELATED MEANINGS

The phrasal verb "do up" has two unrelated meanings.

Mirek did up his coat to keep out the icy breeze.
fasten a piece of clothing

Emily is doing up her house at the moment.
improve, renovate

LITERAL AND METAPHORICAL MEANINGS

Certain phrasal verbs have a basic literal meaning, and a more complicated metaphorical one.

This sentence uses the literal meaning of "break up." The chocolate is being separated into smaller pieces.

Patrick broke up the chocolate before adding it to the cake mixture.
separate something into smaller pieces

In this sentence, nothing has literally broken, but Maria and Pablo have metaphorically separated from each other.

After a huge argument, Maria and Pablo decided to break up.
end a romantic relationship

REGISTER

Although some phrasal verbs can be used in formal situations, others are more informal. Many phrasal verbs have a single-word equivalent which is more formal.

This sentence uses the high-register word "persevere," which is only usually used in formal language.

Despite the storm, the engineers persevered and installed the new phone line.

This sentence means exactly the same thing, but "soldier on" makes the sentence less formal.

Despite the storm, the engineers soldiered on and installed the new phone line.

SEPARABLE PHRASAL VERBS

If a phrasal verb has an object, the object can sometimes go between the verb and the particle. This does not change the meaning. Phrasal verbs that do this are called "separable" phrasal verbs. See page 234 for more examples.

The object can go after the particle.

He is picking up litter.

He is picking litter up.

The object can also go between the verb and the particle.

He is picking it up.

If the object of a separable phrasal verb is a pronoun, it must go between the verb and particle.

FURTHER EXAMPLES

I turned on the light.

I turned the light on.

Can you pick up that box?

Can you pick that box up?

You should throw away those old shoes.

You should throw those old shoes away.

I was annoyed because he woke up the baby.

I was annoyed because he woke her up.

I always fill up the water jug when it's empty.

I always fill it up when it's empty.

⚠ COMMON MISTAKES SEPARABLE PHRASAL VERBS

If the direct object of a separable phrasal verb is a pronoun, it must go between the verb and the particle.

Pronoun

He picked it up. ✓

The pronoun cannot go at the end of the sentence.

He picked up it. ✗

INSEPARABLE PHRASAL VERBS

Some phrasal verbs cannot be separated. The object must always come after the particle—it can never sit between the verb and the particle. This is true whether the object is a noun or a pronoun. See page 235 for more examples.

We had to run to get on the train. ✓

The verb and the particle must stay together.

We had to run to get on it. ✓

The verb and particle stay together even if the direct object is a pronoun.

We had to run to get the train on. ✗

This is wrong. The object cannot sit between the verb and the particle.

FURTHER EXAMPLES

I've come across a new recipe.

He sleeps in most Saturdays.

I need to go over my notes.

I ran into her at the supermarket.

Susan really takes after her father, they're very similar.

Drop by the house any time you like.

SEPARABLE AND INSEPARABLE PHRASAL VERBS

Some phrasal verbs, like "get back from," can be separable or inseparable depending on the context.

When "get back from" means "retrieve from" it is separable. The object must go between "get" and "back."

I finally got my lawnmower back from Dave.

When "get back from" means "return from," it is always inseparable.

I got back from Italy yesterday.

PHRASAL NOUNS

See page 236 for a list of common phrasal nouns.

Some nouns are formed from phrasal verbs, often by joining the verb and the particle together.

Verb — Particle

The teacher asked me to hand out the exam papers.

The teacher gave us a handout for the lesson.

Phrasal noun

Sometimes, the noun is formed by putting the particle in front of the verb.

Oh no! It was sunny and now it's pouring down.

We have a rainy season with daily downpours.

FURTHER EXAMPLES

The company is trying to cut back on staff expenses.

Not another cutback! The company must be in serious trouble.

It's a shame that he wants to drop out of school.

We've had a surprisingly high percentage of dropouts in the class.

We want to get away and go somewhere sunny this winter.

A trip to Australia sounds like a fabulous getaway.

PHRASAL ADJECTIVES

Some adjectives are formed from phrasal verbs, often by joining the verb and the particle together, sometimes with a hyphen.

See page 237 for a list of common phrasal adjectives.

Verb → Particle

Zane asked James to tone down his language.

Zane asked James to use more toned-down language.

Phrasal adjective

Sometimes, the adjective is formed by putting the particle in front of the verb.

Anetta is always speaking out about environmental issues.

Anetta is very outspoken about environmental issues.

FURTHER EXAMPLES

For this yoga position, you have to stretch your arms out.

Simon got into position with his arms outstretched.

Ed watered down his opinion when writing his review.

Ed wrote a watered-down version of his real opinion for the review.

Kemal knocked down the price of jewelry by 15%.

Kemal sold some of his jewelry at a knockdown price.

01 People and things

1.1 PEOPLE

Hundreds of people packed into the town hall to watch the debate.

pack into
fit into a place in large numbers

I found it really hard to fit in with the art class. They're all much younger than me.

fit in (with)
feel like you belong in a group

Some of the older children have been ganging up on me and calling me names.

gang up (on)
form a group to hurt someone

Sheila's neighbors look down on her because her house is smaller than theirs.

look down on
think you are better than another person

I got my son a puppy for his birthday. After asking me for months, he finally wore me down!

wear down
convince someone to do what you want (often by asking many times)

I bumped into Sandra at the park. She was asking after you.

ask after
ask for news about someone

Thousands of fans flooded into the stadium to watch the singer perform.

flood in(to)
enter a space in large numbers

After the concert, everyone spilled out of the stadium and made their way to the train station.

spill out (of)
leave a space in large numbers

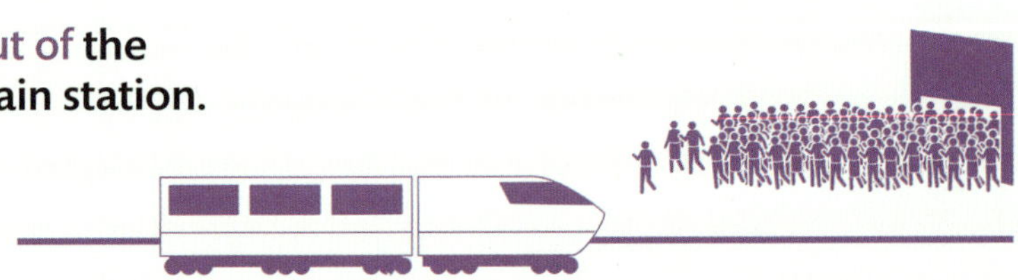

See also:
come across **39**, **52** fit in **15** get back (from) **35**
turn on **27** turn to **13**, **21**, **45**, **50** turn up **4**, **27**

My sister watched over our son while Ania and I went shopping.

watch over
make sure nothing bad happens to someone or something

Adi has got a temper. He turned on me the instant I suggested he buy a new suit.

turn on
attack someone without warning

Toshiro's been buttering his brother up because he wants to borrow his car.

butter up
praise or flatter someone so that they will do you a favor

Jordan's aunts always fuss over him when they come to visit.

fuss over
pay a lot of attention to someone

Barney really looks up to his grandfather. He loves listening to his stories.

look up to
admire someone

1.2 THINGS

Nuwa gathered up the plates from the table and took them to the kitchen.

gather up
collect things together

It was really hard to part with my old car. I'd had it since I was a student.

part with
relinquish something important to you

While looking through things in my attic, I came across an old portrait of my great-grandfather.

come across
find something by chance

Mel lent Dave her lawnmower a month ago, and she finally got it back from him.

get back (from)
retrieve something

Ava lost her passport ages ago. It turned up when she was cleaning the living room.

turn up
be found (usually by accident)

Aa 1.3 READ THE STATEMENTS AND MARK THE CORRECT MEANING

Barney really looks up to his grandfather.
He loves his grandfather. ☐
He admires his grandfather. ☑
He hates his grandfather. ☐

1. After the concert, everyone spilled out of the stadium.
   People entered the stadium together. ☐
   People ran around the stadium together. ☐
   People left the stadium in large numbers. ☐

2. Toshiro's been buttering his brother up.
   He has been flattering him for a favor. ☐
   He has been yelling at him. ☐
   He has been arguing with him. ☐

3. Sheila's arrogant neighbors look down on her.
   They think they are better than her. ☐
   They think she is better than them. ☐
   They think she is wonderful. ☐

4. I came across an old portrait of my great-grandfather.
   I threw away the portrait. ☐
   I found the portrait by chance. ☐
   I looked for the portrait. ☐

Aa 1.4 MATCH THE PICTURES TO THE CORRECT SENTENCES

1. 

2. 

3. 

4. 

- I found it hard to fit in with the art class.
- It was hard to part with my old car.
- Sandra was asking after you at the park.
- Jordan's aunts fuss over him when they visit.
- Nuwa gathered up the plates from the table.

Aa 1.5 CROSS OUT THE INCORRECT WORDS IN EACH SENTENCE

Hundreds of people packed into / ~~over~~ / ~~through~~ the town hall to watch the debate.

1. Some of the older children have been **mobbing** / **ganging** / **teaming** up on me and calling me names.
2. Ava lost her passport ages ago. It turned **out** / **on** / **up** when she was cleaning the living room.
3. Adi has got a temper. He **pivoted** / **turned** / **rotated** on me the instant I suggested he buy a new suit.
4. Mel lent Dave her lawnmower a month ago, and she finally got it **back** / **forward** / **down** from him.

Aa 1.6 WRITE THE CORRECT PHRASAL VERB NEXT TO ITS DEFINITION

retrieve something = *get back (from)*

1. be found (usually by accident) = ____________
2. make sure nothing bad happens to someone = ____________
3. attack someone without warning = ____________
4. convince someone to do what you want = ____________
5. fit into a place in large numbers = ____________

watch over | turn up | wear down | pack into | ~~get back (from)~~ | turn on

1.7 LISTEN TO THE AUDIO AND COMPLETE THE SENTENCES BELOW THE IMAGES

Thousands of fans *flooded into* the stadium.

3. I got my son a puppy. After asking me for months, he finally ________ me ________ !

1. Some of the older children have been ____________ on me and calling me names.

4. Hundreds of people ____________ the town hall to watch the debate.

2. Mel lent Dave her lawnmower a month ago, and she finally ________ it ________ from him.

5. Barney really ____________ his grandfather. He loves listening to his stories.

02 Family

2.1 FAMILY

Dan and Sheila have brought up their children to be kind to animals.

bring up
teach children how to behave

Liam gets on very well with his elder sister. They're always laughing together.

get on (with)
have a good relationship with someone

Colin lives with his son in a house at the edge of town.

live with
share the same house

Sam wants to be a pilot when he grows up.

grow up
develop from child to adult

Jenny's grown out of her old toys. She prefers playing video games now.

grow out of
lose interest in something as you get older

Albert's parents named him after his great-grandfather.

name after
give someone the same name as someone else

2.2 PETS

Lisa puts her rabbit in its cage each evening before bed.

put in
place inside

Fiona's cat doesn't like strangers, but he's warming to Dan.

warm to
become fond of

I let the cat out every morning after I've woken up.

let out
allow to leave

I let the cat in when it started to rain.

let in
allow to enter

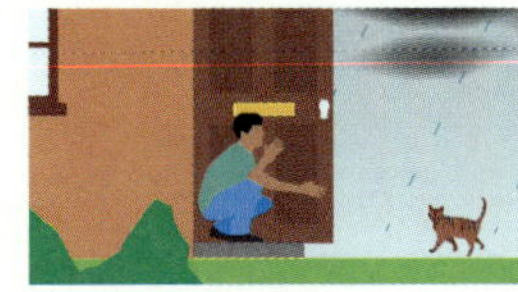

See also:
get on **9**, **15** grow out of **6** let out **6**
live with **47** settle down **45**

After traveling for a few years, Bill settled down and bought a house next door to his parents.

settle down
live in one place

My family pulled together when my father was unwell.

pull together
work as a group to deal with a difficult situation

My mother looks after my children while I'm at work.

look after
care for, take responsibility for

Will and Joe are identical twins. It's almost impossible to tell them apart.

tell apart
recognize the difference

Jasmine takes after her mother. They're very similar people.

take after
have the characteristics of a parent or relative

Whenever his children stay out late, Carlo waits up until they get home.

wait up
wait for someone to get home before going to bed

Olly's dog ran away last week while they were at the park.

run away
escape

After a few days, Olly's dog came back all by herself.

come back
return

Aa 2.3 MATCH THE PICTURES TO THE CORRECT SENTENCES

1 

2 

3 

Olly's dog ran away last week while they were at the park.

My family pulled together when my father was unwell.

My mother looks after my children while I'm at work.

I let the cat in when it started to rain.

Aa 2.4 MARK THE SENTENCES THAT ARE CORRECT

My mother looks after my children while I'm at work. ☑

My mother looks over my children while I'm at work. ☐

1. After a few days, Olly's dog came back all by herself. ☐
   After a few days, Olly's dog came under all by herself. ☐

2. Jasmine takes over her mother. They're very similar people. ☐
   Jasmine takes after her mother. They're very similar people. ☐

3. I let the cat around every morning after I've woken up. ☐
   I let the cat out every morning after I've woken up. ☐

4. Albert's parents named him after his great-grandfather. ☐
   Albert's parents named him behind his great-grandfather. ☐

5. After traveling for a few years, Bill settled up and bought a house. ☐
   After traveling for a few years, Bill settled down and bought a house. ☐

6. Colin lives on his son in a house at the edge of town. ☐
   Colin lives with his son in a house at the edge of town. ☐

2.5 FILL IN THE GAPS USING THE WORDS IN THE PANEL

Olly's dog ran ___away___ last week while they were at the park.

1. Lisa puts her rabbit ______ its cage each evening before bed.
2. Will and Joe are identical twins. It's almost impossible to tell them ______ .
3. After traveling for a few years, Bill settled ______ and bought a house next door to his parents.
4. Liam gets ______ very well with his elder sister. They're always laughing together.
5. Fiona's cat doesn't like strangers, but he's warming ______ Dan.
6. Jenny's grown ______ of her old toys, she prefers playing video games now.

to	down	~~away~~	on	apart	out	in

2.6 LISTEN TO THE AUDIO AND COMPLETE THE SENTENCES BELOW THE IMAGES

Sam wants to be a pilot when he ___grows up___ .

1. Will and Joe are identical twins. It's almost impossible to ______ them ______ .

2. Lisa ______ her rabbit ______ its cage each evening before bed.

3. Jasmine ______ her mother. They're very similar people.

4. I ______ the cat ______ every morning after I've woken up.

5. Jenny's ______ her old toys, she prefers playing video games now.

03 Relationships

3.1 FRIENDSHIPS

Our shared interest in music has really brought us together.

bring together
create a close relationship

I've really gone off Paul since I saw him at the party. He behaved very badly.

go off
like something or someone less

Ken stuck by Cath when her restaurant went bankrupt.

stick by
continue to support someone who is in a difficult situation

Misha stood by Colin when he decided to quit college.

stand by
support or defend someone when other people don't

3.2 ROMANTIC RELATIONSHIPS

Jack and Ula really care for each other. They've been together for 50 years.

care for
love someone or like them very much

Sonia is trying to win Claude back because she's still in love with him.

win back
persuade someone to start having a romantic relationship with you again

I think Pierre has fallen for Clara. Have you seen how he looks at her?

fall for
start loving someone, fall in love

My brother set me up with a woman who works at his office.

set up
arrange a date for someone else

Luisa has finished with Ben. He's very upset.

finish with (UK)
end a relationship with someone

They started going out with each other when they were at school.

go out (with)
have a romantic relationship with someone

See also:
break up **15**, **21**, **29**, **38** care for **32** fall for **41** go off **8**, **27**, **30**, **35**
go out **5**, **27**, **54** set up **12**, **53** take out **14**, **21**, **28**

After we left school, my friends and I drifted apart. I became more interested in my career than music.

drift apart
slowly become less close

Although I haven't seen Zaira for many years, I always hear from her on my birthday.

hear from
receive news from

My best friends and I have stuck together since high school.

stick together
stay together and support each other

Bernadette confided in Martha that she was in love with Pavel.

confide in
share a secret with someone you trust

Katia and I dated for a few weeks, but our relationship fizzled out.

fizzle out
lose energy over a period of time, slowly come to an end

Robin asked Helen out yesterday. They're going to the movies together.

ask out
invite someone to go on a date with you

For our first date, Phil took me out to an expensive restaurant.

take out
take someone on a date

After a huge argument, Maria and Pablo decided to break up.

break up (with)
end a romantic relationship

Carlos and Mia separated a few months ago, but they recently got back together.

get back together
restart a romantic relationship

3.3 LISTEN TO THE AUDIO, THEN NUMBER THE SENTENCES IN THE ORDER YOU HEAR THEM

A Robin asked Helen out yesterday. They're going to the movies together. ☐

B I think Pierre has fallen for Clara. Have you seen how he looks at her? ☐

C Our shared interest in music has really brought us together. [1]

D Carlos and Mia separated a few months ago, but they recently got back together. ☐

E After a huge argument, Maria and Pablo decided to break up. ☐

F Although I haven't seen Zaira for many years, I always hear from her on my birthday. ☐

3.4 FILL IN THE GAPS, PUTTING THE WORDS IN THE CORRECT ORDER

up | to | break

After a huge argument, Maria and Pablo decided *to* *break* *up*.

me | up | set

1 My brother ____ ____ ____ with a woman who works at his office.

for | care | really

2 Jack and Ula ____ ____ ____ each other. They've been together for 50 years.

with | going | out

3 They started ____ ____ ____ each other when they were at school.

by | stood | Colin

4 Misha ____ ____ ____ when he decided to quit college.

Aa 3.5 MATCH THE DEFINITIONS TO THE CORRECT PHRASAL VERBS

	start loving someone, fall in love	→	fall for
1	like something or someone less		fizzle out
2	create a close relationship		drift apart
3	slowly come to an end		fall for
4	arrange a date for someone else		finish with
5	slowly become less close		bring together
6	end a relationship with someone		care for
7	love someone or like them very much		go off
			set up

Aa 3.6 LOOK AT THE PICTURES AND COMPLETE THE SENTENCES USING PHRASAL VERBS

Katia and I dated for a few weeks, but our relationship *fizzled out*.

1 My best friends and I have ____________ since high school.

2 For our first date, Phil ________ me ________ to an expensive restaurant.

3 Bernadette ____________ Martha that she was in love with Pavel.

4 Luisa has ____________ Ben. He's very upset.

5 Ken ____________ Cath when her restaurant went bankrupt.

04 Visiting people

4.1 VISITING PEOPLE

I popped in to see Brian on Saturday morning.

pop in (UK)
visit someone at their home (informal)

We chatted for hours, and he suggested I stick around for dinner.

stick around
stay somewhere longer than planned

Angelo turned up at my house at 6am. I was still in bed!

turn up
arrive (often unexpectedly)

After chatting on the doorstep for a moment, Malik invited me in.

invite in(to)
ask someone to enter your house

On our way home from the beach, we called in to see Grandma.

call in (UK)
visit someone at their home (often on your way elsewhere)

Following the interview, the secretary showed Connor out.

show out
take someone to the door as they leave

My new neighbors, Kaito and Leiko, had me over for dinner last night.

have over
have people as guests at your home

They showed me around their beautiful home.

show around
give someone a tour

It looks like Kia has invited everyone she knows along to the party.

invite along (to)
ask someone to go somewhere with you

See also:
call in 22, 50 come in 56
turn up 1, 27

While you're in town, try to swing by. It would be good to see you.

swing by
visit someone's house on your way somewhere else

My father came into the house and took off his coat.

come in(to)
enter a place

Yesterday afternoon, Liam dropped in for a cup of coffee and a chat.

drop in
visit someone at their home (informal)

On her way home from the gym, Miriam stopped off at the supermarket to get something for dinner.

stop off
stop during a journey to do something

While everyone was in the garden, I found Klaus snooping around the kitchen.

snoop around
secretly look for something

4.2 A PARTY INVITATION

Dear Mason and Emily,

We'd like to invite you over for a barbecue to celebrate Beth's birthday on Saturday. Feel free to come over any time after 2pm, and please bring the kids along, too!

Love, Omar and Beth
P.S. You are all welcome to stay over if you like!

We'd like to invite you over for a barbecue to celebrate Beth's birthday.

invite over
invite someone to your home

Omar told us to come over any time after 2pm.

come over
visit someone (at their home)

Mason and Emily brought the kids along to the barbecue.

bring along
bring someone or something with you

We ended up staying over at Beth and Omar's house.

stay over
stay at someone's house overnight

4.3 LISTEN TO THE AUDIO AND MARK THE PHRASAL VERBS YOU HEAR

come into ☑
pop in ☐

1 show around ☐
have over ☐

2 invite along ☐
turn up ☐

3 show out ☐
stop off ☐

4 snoop around ☐
swing by ☐

5 drop in ☐
stay over ☐

4.4 READ THE STATEMENTS AND MARK THE CORRECT MEANING

I popped in to see Brian on Saturday morning.
I called Brian. ☐
I visited Brian at his home. ☑
I invited Brian to my home. ☐

1 Angelo turned up at my house at 6am.
He arrived at 6am. ☐
He left at 6am. ☐
He fell asleep at 6am. ☐

2 They showed me around their beautiful home.
They asked me to leave. ☐
They asked me to come in. ☐
They gave me a tour. ☐

3 Mason and Emily brought the kids along.
They took their kids away. ☐
They left their kids behind. ☐
They brought their kids with them. ☐

4 We'd like to invite you over for a barbecue.
We'd like you to come to our home. ☐
We'd like you to call us. ☐
We'd like you to host a barbecue. ☐

5 Liam dropped in for a cup of coffee and a chat.
He dropped coffee on himself. ☐
He visited me at my home. ☐
He took me out for coffee. ☐

Aa 4.5 MATCH THE BEGINNINGS OF THE SENTENCES TO THE CORRECT ENDINGS

Following the interview, → the secretary showed Connor out.

1. On her way home from the gym,
2. My father came into the house
3. Omar told us to come over
4. After chatting on the doorstep,
5. We ended up staying over
6. While everyone was in the garden,

- and took off his coat.
- I found Klaus snooping around inside.
- the secretary showed Connor out.
- at Beth and Omar's house.
- Miriam stopped off at the supermarket.
- Malik invited me in.
- any time after 2pm.

Aa 4.6 REWRITE THE SENTENCES, CORRECTING THE ERRORS

Yesterday afternoon, Liam **dropped out** for a cup of coffee and a chat.
Yesterday afternoon, Liam dropped in for a cup of coffee and a chat.

1. My new neighbors, Kaito and Leiko, **had** me **under** for dinner last night.

2. We chatted for hours, and he suggested I **stick up** for dinner.

3. On our way home from the beach, we **called out** to see Grandma.

4. Omar told us to **come above** any time after 2pm.

5. While you're in town, try to **swing off**. It would be good to see you.

05 Socializing

5.1 SOCIALIZING

Katie asked Lisa if she wanted to come out to play.

come out
go somewhere with someone

Once a year, my school friends and I go out for a meal together to catch up.

catch up (with)
talk to friends who you have not talked to recently

Chris spends most weekends hanging out with his friends.

hang out (with)
spend time at a certain place with your friends (informal)

As I was leaving for the art exhibition, I asked Joe if he wanted to come along.

come along (with)
accompany someone, go somewhere with someone

Vincent and Maya decided to stay in. They ordered some pizza and watched a movie.

stay in
remain at home

The carnival was amazing. We stayed out until dawn.

stay out
remain away from home until late

5.2 LEAVING

Joe suddenly took off without saying where he was going.

take off
leave (often unexpectedly)

The movie was terrible, so we slipped out halfway through.

slip out
leave without telling people

We headed off to the beach early because we wanted to avoid the crowds.

head off (to)
leave, begin a journey

Neil was turned away from the nightclub because he was wearing casual clothes.

turn away (from)
refuse to let someone enter

See also: come along **31**, **52** come out **12**, **41** get together **53**
go out **3**, **27**, **54** hang out **28** head off (to) **8** slip out **51**
take off **6**, **9**, **22**, **55** turn away **19**

Lots of guests were milling around, waiting for Raj to make his speech.

mill around
slowly move around a room or space (often waiting for something)

Amara let her little sister tag along when she went to the ice rink with her friends.

tag along
go somewhere with someone (often without an invitation)

Fleur and Clare were getting ready to go out for the evening.

go out
go somewhere with someone, socialize with friends

Our local hotel has a large room that it hires out for parties.

hire out (UK)
allow someone to use something in exchange for money

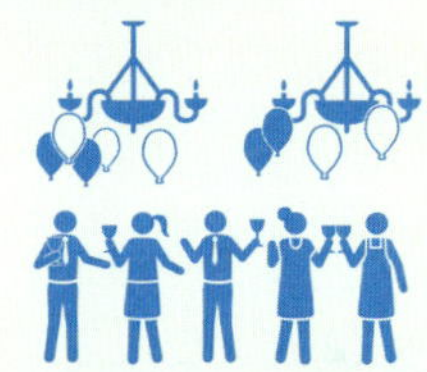

I was glad to see Marvin at the party. He always manages to liven things up.

liven up
make something more exciting

Ella likes to get together with her friends at the ice cream parlor on Friday evenings.

get together
meet and spend time with friends

Charlie stormed out of the store when the manager refused to give him a refund.

storm out (of)
leave somewhere because you are angry

I hate to tear you away, but we're going to miss the last train.

tear away (from)
make someone leave a place even though they want to stay

Paul had to shoot off at the end of the meeting to catch his train home.

shoot off (UK)
leave quickly (informal)

Nadiya had to dash off to pick up the kids from school.

dash off (UK)
leave quickly (informal)

Aa 5.3 CROSS OUT THE INCORRECT WORDS IN EACH SENTENCE

Chris spends most weekends hanging ~~up on~~ / out with / ~~in on~~ his friends.

1 Amara let her little sister tag along / about / above when she went to the ice rink.

2 Ella likes to get under / together / on with her friends at the ice cream parlor.

3 I hate to tear you out / away / up, but we're going to miss the last train.

4 Katie asked Lisa if she wanted to come about / on / out to play.

5 Joe suddenly took off / up / in without saying where he was going.

Aa 5.4 FILL IN THE GAPS USING THE WORDS IN THE PANEL TO CREATE PHRASAL VERBS

Neil was turned *away from* the nightclub because he was wearing casual clothes.

1 Charlie stormed ___ the store when the manager refused to give him a refund.

2 As I was leaving for the art exhibition, I asked Joe if he wanted to come ___ .

3 Lots of guests were milling ___ waiting for Raj to make his speech.

4 Vincent and Maya decided to stay ___ . They ordered pizza and watched a movie.

5 We headed ___ the beach early because we wanted to avoid the crowds.

6 Once a year, my school friends and I go out for a meal together to catch ___ .

along | up | ~~away from~~ | out of | around | off to | in

5.5 LISTEN TO THE AUDIO AND MATCH THE IMAGES TO THE CORRECT PHRASAL VERBS

1 

2 

3 

4 

liven up

catch up

stay out

mill around

shoot off

5.6 FILL IN THE GAPS, PUTTING THE WORDS IN THE CORRECT ORDER

out | through | halfway | slipped

The movie was terrible, so we *slipped* *out* *halfway* *through*.

off | to | dash | pick

1 Nadiya had to ____ ____ ____ ____ up the kids from school.

stayed | We | until | out

2 The carnival was amazing. ____ ____ ____ ____ dawn.

to | ready | out | go

3 Fleur and Clare were getting ____ ____ ____ ____ for the evening.

it | out | hires | for

4 Our local hotel has a large room that ____ ____ ____ ____ parties.

06 Clothing

6.1 CLOTHING

Angelica helped her son to button up his shirt as he got ready for school.

button up
fasten the buttons on a piece of clothing

When Tom realized he was late, he threw on a jacket and tie, and ran for the bus.

throw on
put a piece of clothing on quickly

As Hasan was running across the school yard, one of his shoes came off.

come off
fall off by mistake

All the children at the party had dressed up as dinosaurs.

dress up (as)
wear a costume to look like something

I hope this juice stain comes out when I wash my shirt.

come out (of)
be washed clean (about a stain)

Gemma's shoes go really well with that dress.

go with
look good with another piece of clothing

Arnie's so proud of his new jacket. He's been showing it off to everyone.

show off (to)
show people something you are proud of

Mirek did up his coat to keep out the icy breeze.

do up
fasten a piece of clothing

Carly's shoes are too big for her, but she'll grow into them.

grow into
become big enough to wear an item of clothing

Gio's grown out of his sweater, so he's going to give it to his little brother.

grow out of
become too big for an item of clothing

See also: come off **26**, **52** come out (of) **52** cover up **41**
do up **52** grow out of **2** hang up **38** let out **2** put on **27**, **41**, **55**
take in **51**, **55** take off **5**, **9**, **22**, **55**

This dress is a bit too big. We'll need to take it in a little.

take in
make a piece of clothing smaller

The jacket is too tight. We need to let it out a bit.

let out
make a piece of clothing bigger

Kelly stopped to tie up one of her shoe laces.

tie up
fasten (usually your shoe laces)

It was very hot in the lecture theater, so Mario took off his sweater.

take off
remove (a piece of clothing)

Alex put on her prettiest dress to go out for her wedding anniversary.

put on
wear a piece of clothing

Make sure you wrap up before heading out into that cold weather.

wrap up
wear certain clothes to keep you warm

Maurice hung up his coat as he walked in.

hang up
place a piece of clothing on a hook or hanger

Zane folded up his clothes and put them in the wardrobe.

fold up
make a piece of clothing smaller by folding it neatly

The sun is really strong today, so make sure you cover up.

cover up
protect your skin with clothing

Marlon zipped up his leather jacket and walked toward the door.

zip up
fasten the zipper on a piece of clothing

Aa 6.2 MATCH THE PICTURES TO THE CORRECT SENTENCES

1 

2 

3 

4 

- Angelica helped her son to button up his shirt as he got ready for school.
- As Hasan was running across the school yard, one of his shoes came off.
- All the children at the party had dressed up as dinosaurs.
- I hope this juice stain comes out when I wash my shirt.
- Maurice hung up his coat as he walked in.

Aa 6.3 MARK THE SENTENCES THAT ARE CORRECT

I hope this juice stain comes out when I wash my shirt. ☑
I hope this juice stain comes in when I wash my shirt. ☐

1 Marlon zipped up his leather jacket and walked toward the door. ☐
Marlon zipped down his leather jacket and walked toward the door. ☐

2 Gemma's shoes go really well about that dress. ☐
Gemma's shoes go really well with that dress. ☐

3 Arnie's so proud of his new jacket. He's been showing it on over everyone. ☐
Arnie's so proud of his new jacket. He's been showing it off to everyone. ☐

4 Zane folded up his clothes and put them in the wardrobe. ☐
Zane folded away his clothes and put them in the wardrobe. ☐

6.4 LISTEN TO THE AUDIO, THEN NUMBER THE SENTENCES IN THE ORDER YOU HEAR THEM

A. It was very hot in the lecture theater, so Mario took off his sweater. ☐

B. The jacket is too tight. We need to let it out a bit. ☐

C. All the children at the party had dressed up as dinosaurs. [1]

D. This dress is a bit too big. We'll need to take it in a little. ☐

E. Make sure you wrap up before heading out into that cold weather. ☐

F. When Tom realized he was late, he threw on a jacket and tie, and ran for the bus. ☐

G. Angelica helped her son to button up his shirt as he got ready for school. ☐

6.5 LOOK AT THE PICTURES AND COMPLETE THE SENTENCES USING PHRASAL VERBS

Carly's shoes are too big for her, but she'll ___*grow into*___ them.

3. The sun is really strong today, so make sure you ______________ .

1. Mirek ______________ his coat to keep out the icy breeze.

4. Gio's ______________ his sweater, so he's going to give it to his little brother.

2. Kelly stopped to ______________ one of her shoe laces.

5. Alex ______________ her prettiest dress to go out for her wedding anniversary.

07 Before and after

7.1 CAUSE AND EFFECT

Heavy traffic has impacted badly on the city's air quality.

impact on
have a strong effect on something

Due to her injury, Colleen had to face up to the fact that she couldn't play in the match.

face up to
accept and deal with a bad situation

The heavy rain resulted in floods throughout the city.

result in
cause something to happen

The discovery of some ancient ruins has led to an increase in tourism.

lead to
cause something to happen

Scientists think that an asteroid colliding with Earth caused the dinosaurs to die out.

die out
disappear, become extinct

The invention of the computer brought about the end of the typewriter.

bring about
cause something to happen

7.2 MAKING COMPARISONS

Old cell phones can't compete with today's smartphones.

compete with
be as good as something else

Sanjay got 100% on his exam. He more than measured up to his parents' expectations.

measure up (to)
be as good as people had hoped

To get into college, you'll need to improve on last year's results.

improve on
do something better than before

The new action movie really lived up to the crowd's expectations.

live up to
be as good as people had hoped

Aa 7.3 MATCH UP THE PAIRS OF SENTENCES THAT MEAN THE SAME THING

The heavy rain resulted in floods throughout the city. → The heavy rain caused floods throughout the city.

1. Heavy traffic has impacted badly on the city's air quality.
2. Old cell phones can't compete with today's smartphones.
3. Due to her injury, Colleen had to face up to the fact that she couldn't play in the match.
4. To get into college, you'll need to improve on last year's results.

- Old cell phones aren't as good as today's smartphones.
- The heavy rain caused floods throughout the city.
- Due to her injury, Colleen had to accept the fact that she couldn't play in the match.
- To get into college, you'll need to get better results than you got last year.
- Heavy traffic has had a strong effect on the city's air quality.

7.4 LISTEN TO THE AUDIO AND COMPLETE THE SENTENCES THAT DESCRIBE EACH PICTURE

Scientists think that an asteroid colliding with Earth caused the dinosaurs to *die out*.

1.  Sanjay got 100% on his exam. He more than ______ his parents' expectations.
2.  The new action movie really ______ the crowd's expectations.
3.  The discovery of some ancient ruins has ______ an increase in tourism.
4.  The invention of the computer ______ the end of the typewriter.
5.  The heavy rain ______ floods throughout the city.

08 Everyday life

8.1 DAILY ROUTINE

My alarm goes off at 7am every morning during the week.

go off
begin ringing (about an alarm clock)

Orla went to the bathroom to freshen up before going out.

freshen up
make yourself look clean and tidy

I usually head off to work at 8 in the morning.

head off (to)
leave, begin a journey

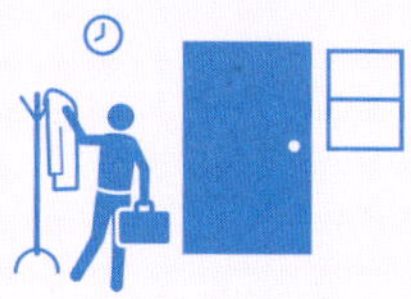

Kieran woke up in the middle of the night when he heard a noise outside.

wake up
stop sleeping, become alert

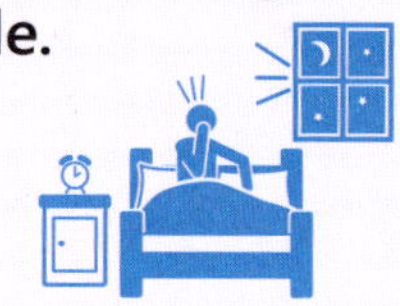

In the evening, I often don't get in until after 7pm.

get in
arrive home

Nico usually gets up at about 10am on Saturdays.

get up
get out of bed

8.4 PHRASAL VERBS ABOUT SLEEP

I tried to wake Mia when I saw she had dozed off at her desk.

doze off
fall asleep, often during the day

On Sunday mornings, I sometimes sleep in as late as 11am.

sleep in
sleep for a longer time than usual

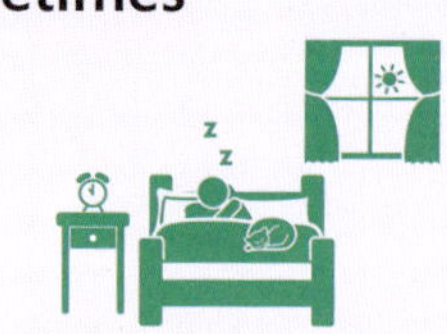

Quite a few people nodded off during the speech.

nod off
fall asleep (without meaning to)

Hanif slept through his alarm again. He's going to be late for work.

sleep through
not wake up when your alarm rings

See also:
drop off **9** get in **9**, **53** get up **53**
go off **3**, **27**, **30**, **35** head off (to) **5**

8.2 RELAXING

When Noel got home from work, he sat down and read a book.

sit down
take a sitting position

Sara was feeling tired, so she lay down on the couch and tried to get some rest.

lie down
take a lying position

Alfred spent the afternoon pottering about in the garden.

potter about
do small tasks in a relaxed way

8.3 TASKS

Once the guests had left, Marco set about doing the dishes.

set about (UK)
begin doing something (with energy or enthusiasm)

After a short break, Ramone got on with cleaning the bathroom.

get on with
concentrate on doing something (usually after a break)

Martina stayed up late revising for her exam the following morning.

stay up
go to bed later than usual

Uma is still sleeping off the effects of the anesthetic. She'll be able to see you soon.

sleep off
sleep to allow you to recover from the effects of a drug

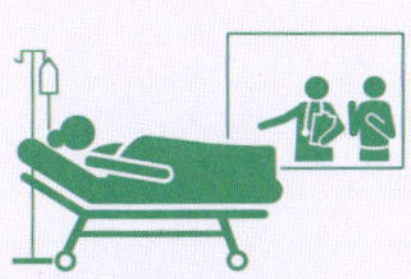

Bradley is sleeping over at his cousin's house tonight. He's so excited about it.

sleep over
sleep at someone else's house (usually about children)

I'm exhausted. I know it's only half past eight, but I'm going to have to turn in.

turn in
go to bed

After a long day at the office, Andrew dropped off in front of the TV.

drop off
fall asleep

Aa 8.5 MATCH THE PHRASAL VERBS TO THE CORRECT DEFINITIONS

	Phrasal verb	Definition
	drop off → fall asleep	do small tasks in a relaxed way
1	sleep through	make yourself look clean and tidy
2	turn in	fall asleep
3	stay up	get out of bed
4	lie down	not wake up when your alarm rings
5	potter about	go to bed
6	freshen up	go to bed later than usual
7	get up	take a lying position

8.6 LISTEN TO THE AUDIO AND MARK THE PHRASAL VERBS YOU HEAR

stay up ☑ doze off ☐

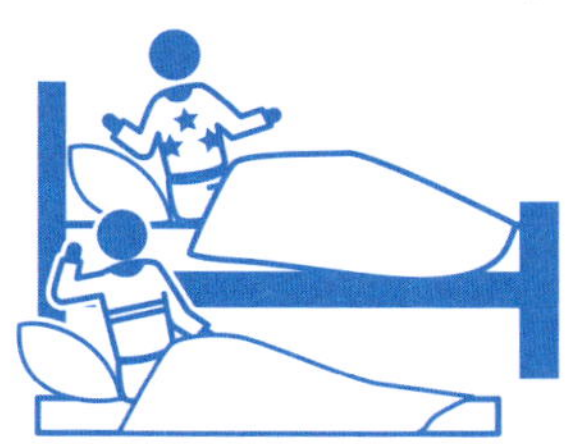

1 sleep over ☐ set about ☐

2 turn in ☐ sleep in ☐

3 freshen up ☐ get in ☐

4 get up ☐ nod off ☐

5 head off ☐ go off ☐

Aa 8.7 WRITE THE PHRASAL VERBS FROM THE PANEL UNDER THE CORRECT DEFINITIONS

fall asleep (without meaning to)

nod off

③ fall asleep, often during the day

❶ stop sleeping, become alert

④ take a sitting position

❷ leave, begin a journey

⑤ begin doing something (with energy or enthusiasm)

wake up | sit down | doze off | set about | ~~nod off~~ | head off (to)

Aa 8.8 FILL IN THE GAPS, PUTTING THE WORDS IN THE CORRECT ORDER

get | don't | in

In the evening, I often *don't* *get* *in* until after 7pm.

on | got | with

❶ After a short break, Ramone ______ ______ ______ cleaning the bathroom.

up | late | stayed

❷ Martina ______ ______ ______ studying for her exam the following morning.

dozed | at | off

❸ I tried to wake Mia when I saw she had ______ ______ ______ her desk.

off | nodded | during

❹ Quite a few people ______ ______ ______ the speech.

09 Transportation

9.1 VEHICLES

Christina's motorcycle broke down while she was traveling through the desert.

break down
stop working

Clive tried to restart the motorboat's engine after it cut out without any warning.

cut out
suddenly stop working

Angelo left his house and got into the taxi.

get in(to)
enter (a car or taxi)

As the movie star got out of the limousine, photographers surrounded him.

get out (of)
exit (a car or taxi)

George and Yolanda got on the train to Paris.

get on
enter (public transportation)

Gina got off the bus when it arrived at her stop.

get off
exit (public transportation)

9.2 DRIVING

George checked the road for other vehicles before driving off.

drive off
drive away, leave

Jen turned back when she realized that she had forgotten her phone.

turn back
return in the direction you have just come from

Tanya turned off the main road and drove along the track to the beach.

turn off
leave a road and drive onto a different one

When you reach the castle, turn onto the highway and head west.

turn onto
join a road from a different one

See also: break down **46**, **50** cut out **37** drop off **8** get in **8**, **53** get off **22** get on **2**, **15** get out **53**, **56** pick up **10**, **11**, **28**, **31**, **38** pull over **13** pull up **28** take off **5**, **6**, **22**, **55** turn off **27**

Kamal dropped me off at the train station on his way to work.

drop off
take a person somewhere in a car and leave them there

Sally picked her friends up outside the movie theater at 9pm.

pick up
go to collect someone (usually in a car)

You should always slow down when you drive past a school.

slow down
go more slowly

The train left the station slowly, before speeding up as it headed to the coast.

speed up
go more quickly

The helicopter took off from the top of the skyscraper.

take off
begin to fly

The plane touched down in Dubai at 9pm in the evening.

touch down
land

We pulled in at a small roadside café, where we could have some breakfast.

pull in(to)
stop and park somewhere

I pulled up by the train station to let my daughter out.

pull up
stop driving (often for a short time)

Marion didn't notice the motorcycle as she pulled out of the junction.

pull out (of)
move from one road to another

I got lost driving to your house. I had to pull over and ask for directions.

pull over
drive to the side of the road and stop

Aa 9.3 MATCH THE PICTURES TO THE CORRECT SENTENCES

1 

2 

3 

4 

5 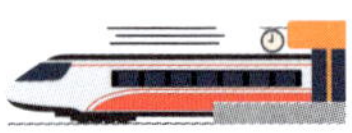

- The helicopter took off from the top of the skyscraper.
- George checked the road for other vehicles before driving off.
- Gina got off the bus when it arrived at her stop.
- I got lost driving to your house. I had to pull over and ask for directions.
- The train left the station slowly, before speeding up as it headed to the coast.
- Tanya turned off the main road and drove along the track to the beach.

Aa 9.4 CROSS OUT THE INCORRECT WORDS IN EACH SENTENCE

Gina got ~~up~~ / off / ~~through~~ the bus when it arrived at her stop.

1. Jen turned down / back / up when she realized that she had forgotten her phone.
2. I pulled up / down / out by the train station to let my daughter out.
3. Sally picked her friends on / in / up outside the movie theater at 9pm.
4. When you reach the castle, turn over / onto / with the highway and head west.
5. Jamie dropped me off / on / in at the train station on his way to work.
6. Angelo left his house and got into / over / up the taxi.
7. Marion didn't notice the motorcycle as she pulled over on / out of / up to the junction.

9.5 LISTEN TO THE AUDIO AND COMPLETE THE SENTENCES THAT DESCRIBE EACH PICTURE

The train left the station slowly, before *speeding up* as it headed to the coast.

3 The plane ______________ in Dubai at 9pm in the evening.

1 As the movie star ______________ the limousine, photographers surrounded him.

4 You should always ______________ when you drive past a school.

2 We ______________ at a small roadside café, where we could have some breakfast.

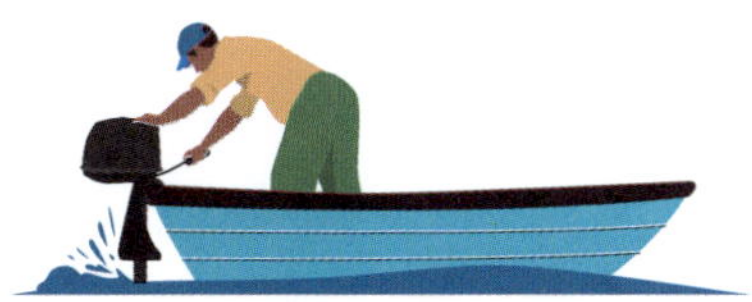

5 Clive tried to restart the motorboat's engine after it ______________ without any warning.

9.6 WRITE THE CORRECT PHRASAL VERB NEXT TO ITS DEFINITION, FILLING IN THE MISSING LETTERS

begin to fly	=	t *a* *k* *e* o *f* *f*
1 enter (public transportation)	=	g _ _ o _
2 go more slowly	=	s _ _ _ d _ _ _
3 stop working	=	b _ _ _ _ d _ _ _
4 drive away, leave	=	d _ _ _ _ o _ _
5 join a road from a different one	=	t _ _ _ o _ _ _

10 Shopping

10.1 SHOPPING

Once Ellie had found a scarf that she liked, she went to **check out**.

check out (US)

pay

Ellie used her credit card to **pay for** the scarf.

pay for

give money for something you are buying

Peter **bought up** all the pizzas in the store before his party.

buy up

buy the entire supply of something

Aziz had been **looking around** the store for ages, but couldn't find a shirt he liked.

look around

visit a place and see what is there

Joshua **crossed off** each item on the shopping list as he found it.

cross off

put a line through a word in a list

Luis put the melon in his basket and **checked** it **off** his shopping list.

check off (US)

put a check mark next to a word in a list

Kemal **knocked down** the price of jewelry by 15% to attract shoppers to his new store.

knock down

reduce prices

I bought my new laptop online, and went to **pick** it **up** at my local store the following day.

pick up

collect an item that you bought online

My favorite author has just **brought out** a new novel.

bring out

put a new product on sale

Fans are **lining up** outside the bookstore to buy it.

line up

wait in a line for something

See also:
check out **35**, **50** pick up **9**, **11**, **28**, **31**, **38**
take back **16**, **44**

Ethan's going camping this weekend, so he's stocking up on insect repellant.

stock up (on)
buy a lot of something in case you need it

The mugs I bought online are broken. I'm going to send them back.

send back
return an item to the seller by mail

Before buying a new car, it's worth shopping around. You might find a bargain.

shop around
visit several stores (or websites) to compare their products and prices

Aisha decided to splash out on clothes for her summer vacation.

splash out (on)
spend a lot of money without thinking too much about it

I went to the market to buy some bread, but they had sold out.

sell out (of)
sell all the available items

Marta couldn't wait to try out her new games console.

try out
try a new product to see what it is like

Carla didn't like the sweater she'd bought, so she decided to take it back.

take back
return a product to the store where you bought it

Shoppers had already snapped up all the bargains at the sale by the time I'd arrived.

snap up
buy something quickly, as soon as it becomes available

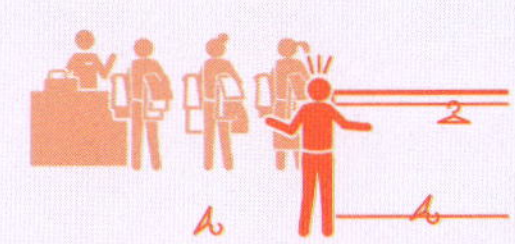

The fitting rooms are over there if you'd like to try it on.

try on
wear an item of clothing to see if it fits

10.2 MATCH UP THE PAIRS OF SENTENCES THAT MEAN THE SAME THING

My favorite author has just brought out a new novel. → My favorite author has just put a new novel on sale.

1 The fitting rooms are over there if you'd like to try it on.

2 The mugs I bought online are broken. I'm going to send them back.

3 I bought my new laptop online, and went to pick it up at my local store.

4 Before buying a new car, it's worth shopping around to find a bargain.

5 I went to the market to buy some bread, but they had sold out.

- The mugs I bought online are broken. I'm going to return them to the seller by mail.
- My favorite author has just put a new novel on sale.
- I went to the market to buy some bread, but all the bread had been sold.
- The fitting rooms are over there if you'd like to wear the clothes to see if they fit.
- I bought my new laptop online, and went to collect it from my local store.
- Before buying a new car, it's worth visiting several stores to compare prices.

10.3 WRITE THE PHRASAL VERBS FROM THE PANEL UNDER THE CORRECT DEFINITIONS

mail an item back to the seller

send back

1 wait in a line for something

______

2 buy a lot of something in case you need it

______

3 put a line through a word in a list

______

4 sell all the available items

______

5 buy something quickly, as soon as it becomes available

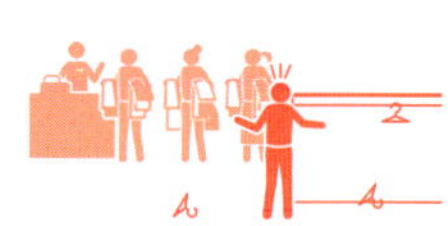

______

cross off | snap up | line up | sell out (of) | ~~send back~~ | stock up (on)

10.4 LISTEN TO THE AUDIO AND COMPLETE THE SENTENCES THAT DESCRIBE EACH PICTURE

Before buying a new car, it's worth *shopping around*. You might find a bargain.

1. 
Marta couldn't wait to ______________ her new games console.

2. 
Kemal ______________ the price of jewelry by 15% to attract shoppers to his new store.

3. 
Luis put the melon in his basket and ______________ his shopping list.

4. 
Aisha decided to ______________ clothes for her summer vacation.

5. 
Ellie used her credit card to ______________ the scarf.

10.5 FILL IN THE GAPS USING THE WORDS IN THE PANEL TO CREATE PHRASAL VERBS

Peter [bought *up*] all the pizzas in the store before his party.

1. Aziz had been [looking ______] the store for ages, but couldn't find a shirt he liked.
2. Shoppers had already [snapped ______] all the bargains at the sale by the time I'd arrived.
3. Once Ellie had found a scarf that she liked, she went to [check ______].
4. Carla didn't like the sweater she'd bought, so she decided to [take it ______].
5. Joshua [crossed ______] each item on the shopping list as he found it.

up	back	~~up~~	off	out	around

11 The weather

11.1 THE WEATHER

As dark storm clouds rolled in from the east, Arthur tried to get home before the rain started.

roll in
(about bad weather) approach, come nearer

It looks like the weather's clearing up. We'll be able to start the game again soon.

clear up
(about weather) improve, become less cloudy

The weather's been awful, but it's finally starting to brighten up.

brighten up
become sunnier, less cloudy

Chris and Mel had to leave the beach when it started bucketing down.

bucket down
rain very heavily (informal)

Once the storm had calmed down, Grace checked her house for damage.

calm down
become less stormy or windy

Minutes after Ben had lit the grill, the sky clouded over. He hoped it wouldn't rain.

cloud over
become more cloudy

Don't go outside yet, Pamela. It's pouring down!

Oh, thanks Martin. I'll wait until it eases off a bit.

pour down
rain heavily

ease off
become less strong or intense

See also:
brighten up **45** calm down **45** clear up **32**, **50**
cool down **11** pick up **9**, **10**, **28**, **31**, **38** warm up **33**

The wind's picking up. It's perfect weather for flying a kite.

pick up
increase, become stronger

As soon as the storm had blown over, the hikers left the cave and continued walking.

blow over
(about a storm) move away

Alice likes to sit on the balcony when the weather cools down in the evening.

cool down
become cooler

After days of bad weather, the rain finally started to let up.

let up
become less severe

People go ice-skating when the lake freezes over in the winter.

freeze over
completely freeze

Ella stood in a bus shelter waiting for the wind to die down.

die down
(about a storm or wind) become calmer

Today started off nicely, so we ate our breakfast on the terrace.

start off
begin

By the end of May, the weather starts to warm up and the tourists start to arrive.

warm up
become warmer

Aa 11.2 MARK THE SENTENCES THAT ARE CORRECT

Don't go outside yet, Pamela. It's pouring down! ☑
Don't go outside yet, Pamela. It's pouring up! ☐

1. Today started off nicely, so we ate our breakfast on the terrace. ☐
   Today started on nicely, so we ate our breakfast on the terrace. ☐

2. After days of bad weather, the rain finally started to let down. ☐
   After days of bad weather, the rain finally started to let up. ☐

3. Chris and Mel had to leave the beach when it started bucketing under. ☐
   Chris and Mel had to leave the beach when it started bucketing down. ☐

4. The weather's been awful, but it's finally starting to brighten up. ☐
   The weather's been awful, but it's finally starting to brighten off. ☐

Aa 11.3 MATCH THE PICTURES TO THE CORRECT SENTENCES

The wind's picking up. It's perfect weather for flying a kite.

1. 

Ella stood in a bus shelter waiting for the wind to die down.

2. 

Minutes after Ben had lit the grill, the sky clouded over.

3. 

People go ice-skating when the lake freezes over in the winter.

4. 

Alice likes to sit on the balcony when the weather cools down in the evening.

Aa 11.4 REWRITE THE SENTENCES, CORRECTING THE ERRORS

Minutes after Ben had lit the grill, the sky **clouded off**. He hoped it wouldn't rain.
Minutes after Ben had lit the grill, the sky clouded over. He hoped it wouldn't rain.

1. As soon as the storm had **blown under**, the hikers left the cave and continued walking.

___

2. As dark storm clouds **rolled out** from the east, Arthur tried to get home before the rain started.

___

3. It looks like the weather's **clearing off**. We'll be able to start the game again soon.

___

4. By the end of May, the weather starts to **warm around** and the tourists start to arrive.

___

5. Once the storm had **calmed up**, Grace checked her house for damage.

___

11.5 LISTEN TO THE AUDIO, THEN NUMBER THE PICTURES IN THE ORDER YOU HEAR THEM

A ☐

B 1

C ☐

D ☐

E ☐

F ☐

G ☐

H ☐

12 Technology

12.1 COMPUTER SYSTEMS

To access your account, log in with your username and password.

log in(to)
enter an account or system

Always make sure you log out of your account after using it, so hackers can't steal your data.

log out (of)
leave an account or system

As soon as Sherelle gets into work, she boots up her computer.

boot up (UK)
(about a computer) start, turn on

You should shut down your computer at night to save electricity.

shut down
(about a computer) turn off

This is the third time that our system has gone down this morning!

go down
(about a network) stop working

I back up all my photos in case my computer breaks. I keep them on an external hard drive.

back up
make a copy of something

Some criminals hacked into our computer system and stole the new designs.

hack into
access a computer or network illegally

Our company hired a technician to set up the new printer.

set up
get something ready to use

12.3 NEW PRODUCTS

My office has started rolling out some new software. People are very confused by it.

roll out
(about a product) introduce

The new phone model came out today. There was a long line outside the store.

come out
(about a product) be released

See also:
back up **44** come out **5**, **6**, **12**, **41**, **52**
go down **32**, **54** set up **3**, **53**

12.2 USING TECHNOLOGY

Pete scrolled up to the top of the document to find the company's address.

scroll up (to)
move toward the top (of a page)

I had to scroll down to the bottom of the page to find the information I was looking for.

scroll down (to)
move toward the bottom (of a page)

When Amy zoomed in, she noticed the red car in front of the restaurant.

zoom in
get a closer view of something

Amy zoomed out to look at the whole picture.

zoom out
get a more distant view of something

You have to type in your password to access the website.

type in
enter information using a keyboard

I type out my essays because it's quicker than writing them by hand.

type out
write a piece of text using a keyboard

If you click on the link at the bottom of the page, you will see the answers.

click on
select something on a computer screen

I printed out a copy of the contract for the clients to sign.

print out
make a paper copy of a text

phase in
(about a product) introduce slowly

phase out
(about a product) replace slowly

12.4 LISTEN TO THE AUDIO, THEN NUMBER THE SENTENCES IN THE ORDER YOU HEAR THEM

A As soon as Sherelle gets into work, she boots up her computer. ☐

B When Amy zoomed in, she noticed the red car in front of the restaurant. 1

C I had to scroll down to the bottom of the page to find the information I was looking for. ☐

D I printed out a copy of the contract for the clients to sign. ☐

E This is the third time that our system has gone down this morning! ☐

F The new phone model came out today. There was a long line outside the store. ☐

G To access your account, log in with your username and password. ☐

12.5 MATCH THE PICTURES TO THE CORRECT SENTENCES

1 

2 

3 

Some criminals hacked into our computer system and stole the new designs.

My office has started rolling out some new software. People are very confused by it.

Pete scrolled up to the top of the document to find the company's address.

When Amy zoomed in, she noticed the red car in front of the restaurant.

Aa 12.6 FILL IN THE GAPS USING THE PHRASAL VERBS IN THE PANEL

This is the third time that our system has *gone down* this morning!

1. You should ________________ your computer at night to save electricity.
2. ________________ the link at the bottom of the page to see the answers.
3. I ________________ all my photos in case my computer breaks.
4. Always make sure you ________________ of your account after using it.
5. The company has started ________________ new computers. They look great!

click on
log out
phasing in
~~gone down~~
shut down
back up

Aa 12.7 REWRITE THE SENTENCES, CORRECTING THE ERRORS

To access your account, **log off** with your username and password.
To access your account, log in with your username and password.

1. I **type in** my essays because it's quicker than writing them by hand.

____

2. I **printed up** a copy of the contract for the clients to sign.

____

3. Our company hired a technician to **put up** the new printer.

____

4. You have to **type down** your password to access the website.

____

5. Amy **zoomed up** to look at the whole picture at once.

____

13 Crime, the law, and politics

13.1 CRIME AND THE LAW

Gustav broke out of prison by digging a hole under the main wall.

break out (of)
escape from a prison

Someone broke into my house and stole all my jewelry.

break in(to)
enter a building to steal something

Phil had to go to the hospital after somebody beat him up.

beat up
injure someone by hitting them repeatedly

The police ordered the criminal to hand over the stolen money.

hand over
return something to its owner

The police are cracking down on illegal parking in the city.

crack down (on)
become stricter about existing rules

Janice is leading a campaign to stamp out littering in the park.

stamp out
make something bad or unpleasant stop happening

The police cordoned off the area where the crime had taken place.

cordon off
use a barrier to stop people from entering an area

Dan tipped off the police about the location of the stolen artworks.

tip off
give someone information anonymously

After robbing the store, the thieves got away in a stolen car.

get away
escape

The police could tell from the tire tracks that the thieves had escaped by car.

tell from
draw a conclusion from evidence

See also:
get away **35** pull over **9**
turn to **21**, **45**, **50**

The local government has brought in a new law banning cars from entering the city center.

bring in
introduce a new law

Watch out for pickpockets when you're on the train!

watch out for
be aware of potential danger

While I was driving home, the traffic police pulled me over for speeding.

pull over
make a driver stop for doing something illegal

The detectives tracked down the thief using fingerprints on the door handle.

track down
work to find something or someone

My brother turned to crime after he lost his job.

turn to
start doing something different

13.2 POLITICS

Activists are calling on the government to protect the country's forests.

call on
ask someone publicly to do something

Senators voted on the new law after a long debate.

vote on
make a decision about a law using a vote

The protestors are calling for better public transportation in the town.

call for
ask publicly for something to happen

One of my old school friends is running for mayor.

run for
be a candidate for a political position

I'm definitely going to vote for her.

vote for
support something or someone by using a vote

13.3 MATCH UP THE PAIRS OF SENTENCES THAT MEAN THE SAME THING

Someone broke into my house and stole all my jewelry. → Someone entered my house without permission and stole all my jewelry.

1. One of my old school friends is running for mayor.
2. The police cordoned off the area where the crime had taken place.
3. After robbing the store, the thieves got away in a stolen car.
4. Watch out for pickpockets when you're on the train!
5. The police are cracking down on illegal parking in the city.
6. Activists are calling on the government to protect the country's forests.

- The police stopped people from entering the area where the crime had taken place.
- Someone entered my house without permission and stole all my jewelry.
- The police are becoming stricter on illegal parking in the city.
- Be aware of pickpockets when you're on the train!
- Activists are asking the government publicly to protect the country's forests.
- One of my old school friends is a candidate for mayor.
- After robbing the store, the thieves escaped in a stolen car.

13.4 LISTEN TO THE AUDIO, THEN NUMBER THE PICTURES IN THE ORDER YOU HEAR THEM

A ☐

B 1

C ☐

D ☐

E ☐

F ☐

G ☐

H ☐

Aa 13.5 MARK THE SENTENCES THAT ARE CORRECT

Gustav broke out of prison by digging a hole under the main wall. ☑
Gustav smashed out of prison by digging a hole under the main wall. ☐

1 

The police ordered the criminal to foot over the stolen money. ☐
The police ordered the criminal to hand over the stolen money. ☐

2 

Senators voted on the new law after a long debate. ☐
Senators voted about the new law after a long debate. ☐

3 

Janice is leading a campaign to stamp out littering in the park. ☐
Janice is leading a campaign to stamp on littering in the park. ☐

4 

While I was driving home, the traffic police grabbed me over for speeding. ☐
While I was driving home, the traffic police pulled me over for speeding. ☐

5 

Dan tipped off the police about the location of the stolen artworks. ☐
Dan tipped up the police about the location of the stolen artworks. ☐

Aa 13.6 WRITE THE CORRECT PHRASAL VERB NEXT TO ITS DEFINITION

draw a conclusion from evidence = *tell from*

1. support something or someone by using a vote = ______________
2. start doing something different = ______________
3. work to find something or someone = ______________
4. injure someone by hitting them repeatedly = ______________
5. introduce a new law = ______________
6. ask publicly for something to happen = ______________

14 Money

14.1 MONEY

Dan has owed me £200 for six months, but he's finally paid up.

pay up
return (usually unwillingly) all the money you have borrowed

I've decided to cut back on spending by bringing my own lunch to work.

cut back (on)
reduce the amount of money you spend

I came into a lot of money when my grandfather died.

come into
receive suddenly; inherit

Sara has finally coughed up the money I lent her last year.

cough up
give money you owe (reluctantly)

I lent Jenny $20 yesterday and she paid me back today.

pay back
return the money you have borrowed

Tommy had to fork out more than $600 to get his car repaired.

fork out (for)
spend a lot of money on something

Nura asked Craig's friends to chip in $5 each toward his birthday present.

chip in
each contribute money

More than a million dollars was wiped off the price of our company this morning.

wipe off
reduce in value

Gary lives off the money that he inherited from his aunt. He does not need to work.

live off
get enough money from somewhere to pay for all the things you need

I try to live on half my paycheck every month so I can save the rest.

live on
have a limited amount of money to buy the things you need

See also:
add up **25**, **41** come to **24** cut back **28** pay off **26**
run into **26** take out **3**, **21**, **28** wipe off **21**

The cost of the new stadium has already run into the millions.

run into
allow a debt or bill to increase to a certain amount

Tara and Ali are saving up for a new house. They try to save $300 each month.

save up
save money (for something in particular)

Try to pay your bills as soon as they arrive. They can soon add up.

add up
accumulate, build up

Patrick went to the bank to pay in some cash.

pay in(to)
put money in a bank

Pete went to the ATM to take out some cash.

take out
withdraw money from a bank

Nick doesn't earn much money, but it's enough to get by.

get by
have just enough money to survive

The food was excellent, but we were shocked when the bill came to more than $200.

come to
reach a certain amount

Wayne paid for everyone's lunches yesterday, so we settled up with him today.

settle up (with)
pay someone what you owe them

Colin has run up some huge debts renovating his house.

run up
allow a debt or bill to increase

He doesn't know how he's going to pay them off.

pay off
finish giving back the money you have borrowed

Aa 14.2 READ THE STATEMENTS AND MARK THE CORRECT MEANING

I lent Jenny $20 yesterday and she paid me back today.

Jenny threw away $20. ☐
Jenny returned $20 to me. ☑
Jenny stole $20 from me. ☐

1 More than a million dollars was wiped off the price of our company this morning.

The company reduced in value. ☐
The company rose in value. ☐
The company shut down. ☐

2 Tommy had to fork out more than $600 to get his car repaired.

Tommy had to spend a lot of money. ☐
Tommy had to save a lot of money. ☐
Tommy had to borrow money. ☐

3 I came into a lot of money when my grandfather died.

I lost a lot of money. ☐
I inherited a lot of money. ☐
I gave away a lot of money. ☐

4 Patrick went to the bank to pay in some cash.

Patrick took money from a bank. ☐
Patrick put money into a bank. ☐
Patrick robbed a bank. ☐

5 Wayne paid for everyone's lunches yesterday, so we settled up with him today.

We took money from Wayne. ☐
We shared money with Wayne. ☐
We paid Wayne what we owed him. ☐

Aa 14.3 WRITE THE PHRASAL VERBS FROM THE PANEL UNDER THE CORRECT DEFINITIONS

have just enough money to survive

get by

1 return all the money you have borrowed (usually unwillingly)

______

2 reduce in value

______

3 allow a debt or bill to increase

______

4 each contribute money

______

5 have a limited amount of money to buy the things you need

______

6 save money (for something in particular)

______

pay up ~~get by~~ live on run up
chip in save up wipe off

Aa 14.4 REWRITE THE SENTENCES, CORRECTING THE ERRORS

He doesn't know how he's going to **pay** them **over**.

He doesn't know how he's going to pay them off.

1. Sara has finally **coughed on** the money I lent her last year.

____

2. I've decided to **cut down for** spending by bringing my own lunch to work.

____

3. The food was excellent, but we were shocked when the bill **went to** more than $200.

____

4. The cost of the new stadium has already **run through** the millions.

____

5. Try to pay your bills as soon as they arrive. They can soon **add on**.

____

14.5 LISTEN TO THE AUDIO AND WRITE THE SENTENCES BELOW THE IMAGES

Gary lives off the money that he inherited.

1. ______________________________

2. ______________________________

3. ______________________________

4. ______________________________

5. ______________________________

15 Time

15.1 TIME

The journey dragged on **for hours. The kids were so bored!**

drag on
continue for a long time (negative)

Mikhail dragged out **his speech for so long that some of the audience fell asleep.**

drag out
make something last too long (negative)

Time's getting on **now. Let's hurry home before it gets dark.**

get on (UK)
become late (about the time)

As the years went by**, I grew to love Phil's sense of humor.**

go by
pass (about time)

We take the children to the park every afternoon to break up **the day.**

break up
break (a day or period of time) into separate parts

The deadline for the project crept up on **us.**

creep up (on)
happen slowly to someone without them noticing it

The doctor's busy at the moment, but I'll try to fit **you** in **later today.**

fit in
make time for something

I enjoy whiling away **the hours reading novels and comic books.**

while away
pass the time in a relaxed way

15.2 WAITING

Hi Sally! Can you hang on **a minute while I grab my umbrella?**

hang on
wait for a short time (informal)

The service here is terrible! It's holding **everyone** up**.**

hold up
make someone or something late

See also:
break up **3**, **21**, **29**, **38** creep up on **51** fit in **15**
get on **2**, **9** go by **54** run out (of) **30** take up **31**, **55**

Danny wasn't able to finish the exam because he ran out of time.

run out (of)
have no more (time)

Hurry up, Oliver! The train's going to leave soon!

hurry up
move or do something more quickly

Cleaning the house took up all of Liam's weekend.

take up
occupy, use up (someone's time)

I can't believe how quickly winter's come around again!

come around
happen again (about a regular event)

Your session has timed out. Please log in again.

time out
log someone out of a computer, server, or website because of inactivity

Our professor always draws out our lectures by answering lots of questions at the end.

draw out
make something last longer than necessary

Commuting to and from work really eats into my time.

eat into
take up too much (of someone's time)

Quitting my job at the café has freed up more time for my studies.

free up
make more time available

Chris was sitting in the café waiting for his girlfriend to arrive.

wait for
stay somewhere or delay something until something happens

When the train was canceled, the passengers had to wait around for the next one.

wait around (for)
do nothing until something happens

Aa 15.3 READ THE STATEMENTS AND MARK THE CORRECT MEANING

Winter's come around again so quickly!
Winter is over. ☐
Winter has started again. ☑
Winter is yet to begin. ☐

1. Hurry up, Oliver! The train's going to leave soon!
   Slow down, Oliver. ☐
   Stop walking, Oliver. ☐
   Move more quickly, Oliver. ☐

2. Quitting my job has freed up time for my studies.
   I have more time for my studies. ☐
   I have less time for my studies. ☐
   I have no time for my studies. ☐

3. As the years went by, I grew to love Phil.
   I began to love Phil. ☐
   I do not love Phil. ☐
   I have always loved Phil. ☐

4. Our professor always draws out our lectures.
   He keeps lectures short. ☐
   He makes lectures last longer. ☐
   He refuses to give lectures. ☐

5. I enjoy whiling away the hours reading.
   I read very fast. ☐
   I read for very little time. ☐
   I like to pass the time by reading. ☐

6. He ran out of time and could not finish the exam.
   He was given more time. ☐
   He had no more time. ☐
   He had some time left. ☐

7. Your session has timed out. Please log in again.
   Your session has ended due to inactivity. ☐
   Your session is still in progress. ☐
   Your session has not begun. ☐

15.4 LISTEN TO THE AUDIO AND MARK THE PHRASAL VERBS YOU HEAR

free up ☑ free down ☐

1. drag out ☐ drag in ☐

2. hurry in ☐ hurry up ☐

3. wait out ☐ wait for ☐

4. break up ☐ break in ☐

5. while over ☐ while away ☐

Aa 15.5 FILL IN THE GAPS USING THE PHRASAL VERBS IN THE PANEL

As the years *went by*, I grew to love Phil's sense of humor. 

1. The journey ______________ for hours. The kids were so bored. 
2. Commuting to and from work really ______________ my time. 
3. Cleaning the house ______________ all of Liam's weekend. 
4. The deadline for the project ______________ us. 

eats into
crept up on
~~went by~~
took up
dragged on

Aa 15.6 FILL IN THE GAPS, PUTTING THE WORDS IN THE CORRECT ORDER

wait | for | around

Passengers had to *wait* *around* *for* the next train.

up | everyone | holding

1. The service here is terrible! It's ________ ________ ________ .

on | now | getting

2. Time's ________ ________ ________ . Let's hurry home before it gets dark.

a | hang | on

3. Can you ________ ________ ________ minute while I grab my umbrella?

fit | in | you

4. The doctor's busy today, but I'll try to ________ ________ ________ tomorrow.

16 Past and future

16.1 FUTURE

The building project has just begun. Months of construction work lie ahead before it'll be finished.

lie ahead
be in the future

Elly and George are looking forward to going to the beach later.

look forward to
wait for something with excitement

All the streets were decorated in the weeks leading up to the festival.

lead up to
happen in the period before an event

Colin is working hard because the deadline for his article is coming up.

come up
approach, happen soon

Kira had dreamed of becoming a great actor, but her plans didn't pan out.

pan out
develop, become successful

16.2 MEMORY

Being at the beach stirs up memories of vacations with my grandmother.

stir up
make someone think about the past

Roland looks back on his college days with pleasure.

look back (on)
remember, think about the past

Finding my old toys brought back happy memories of my childhood.

bring back
make someone think about the past

16.3 CHANGE AND RESCHEDULING

The house was turned into a convenience store in the 1980s.

turn into
become, transform into

We are planning to turn it back into a house and live there.

turn back into
return to its original form

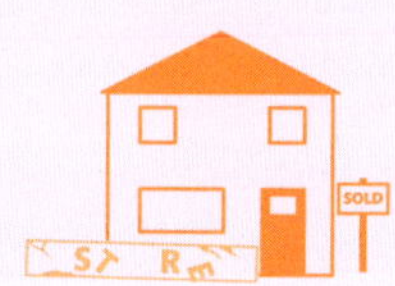

See also:
bring back **35** come up **36**, **50**, **52** go back **35**, **54**
push back **43** take back **10**, **44**

When I recognized Roshan, memories of our days in Delhi came flooding back.

flood back
suddenly come into someone's mind (about memories or emotions)

Peter reminds me of you when you were a little boy.

remind of
make someone remember a person, place, or event from the past

I like to listen to music and think back to my days as a musician in Paris.

think back (to)
think about an event in the past

This dress takes me back to my childhood in the 1960s.

take back (to)
make someone think about the past

Many of the buildings in my city date back to the 19th century.

date back to
come into being at a particular time in the past

The doctor's off this afternoon, so could we bring your appointment forward to 11 o'clock this morning?

bring forward (to)
move to an earlier time

Claude is unwell today. We'll have to push our meeting back to tomorrow.

push back (to)
move an appointment to a later date, postpone

In my country, the clocks go forward one hour in the spring.

go forward
move forward

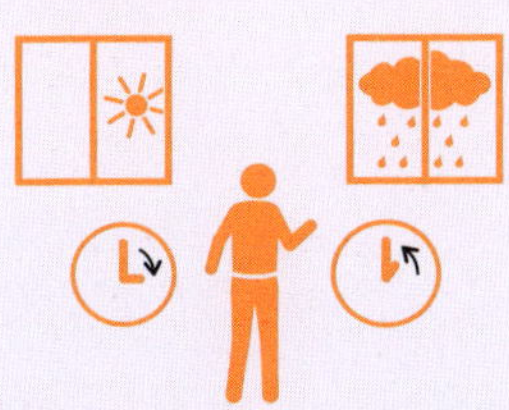

The clocks go back one hour in the fall.

go back
move backward

16.4 LISTEN TO THE AUDIO, THEN NUMBER THE PICTURES IN THE ORDER YOU HEAR THEM

A ☐

B 1

C ☐

D ☐

E ☐

F ☐

G ☐

H ☐

16.5 CROSS OUT THE INCORRECT WORDS IN EACH SENTENCE

The house was turned ~~out~~ / into / ~~over~~ a convenience store in the 1980s.

1. In my country, the clocks go forward / away / under one hour in the spring.
2. The clocks go back to / again in / back one hour in the fall.
3. Elly and George are looking on to / out of / forward to going to the beach later.
4. Claude is unwell today. We'll have to push our meeting back away / to / out tomorrow.
5. Finding my old toys brought back / over / in happy memories of my childhood.
6. The building project has just begun. Months of construction work lie ahead / under / above.
7. We are planning to turn the store back around / over / into a house and live there.
8. All the streets were decorated in the weeks leading up / down / over to the festival.

Aa 16.6 MATCH THE BEGINNINGS OF THE SENTENCES TO THE CORRECT ENDINGS

Being at the beach stirs up memories → of vacations with my grandmother.

1. This dress takes me back to
2. Kira had dreamed of becoming a
3. Peter reminds me of you
4. Many of the buildings in my city
5. The house was turned into

- my childhood in the 1960s.
- when you were a little boy.
- of vacations with my grandmother.
- a convenience store in the 1980s.
- great actor, but her plans didn't pan out.
- date back to the 19th century.

Aa 16.7 REWRITE THE SENTENCES, CORRECTING THE ERRORS

Many of the buildings in my city **date back on** the 19th century.

Many of the buildings in my city date back to the 19th century.

1. The doctor's off tomorrow, so could we **bring** your appointment **forward on** today?

2. Colin is working hard because the deadline for his article is **coming down**.

3. Roland **looks out on** his college days with pleasure.

4. All the streets were decorated in the weeks **leading over to** the festival.

5. I like to listen to music and **think forward to** my days as a musician in Paris.

6. The building project has just begun. Months of construction work **lie before**.

17 Making plans

17.1 MAKING PLANS

Kwang had been planning to study medicine, but ended up studying French.

end up
do something different to what you had originally planned

My dad wanted to buy a motorcycle for ages, but I never expected him to go through with it.

go through with
do something you have planned to do (after some thought or discussion)

The negotiating teams stayed up until after midnight hammering out a new treaty.

hammer out
reach an agreement after much discussion

We want to get married in summer, but we haven't pinned down a location yet.

pin down
decide the details about something

I asked Sabrina if she wanted to go camping, but she threw out the idea.

throw out
reject a suggestion or idea

Giovanni forgot about the art project, but he managed to throw something together.

throw together
do something without preparation

17.2 CANCELING PLANS

Ed had promised to do a bungee jump with me, but backed out at the last minute.

back out
not do something you had agreed to do

Dexter was going to ask Becky out on a date, but he chickened out.

chicken out
decide not to do something you had planned to do because you are afraid (informal)

Adi always manages to wriggle out of helping with the cleaning.

wriggle out of
avoid doing something you should do (informal)

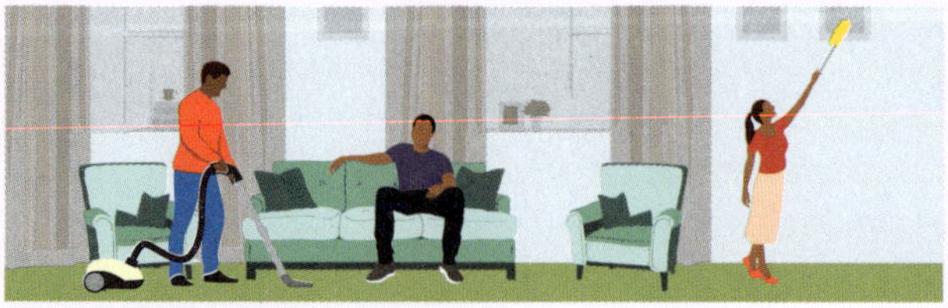

See also:
end up **35** get out of **31**
throw out **39**

You should plan ahead before setting off on a long car journey.

plan ahead
make plans before an event happens

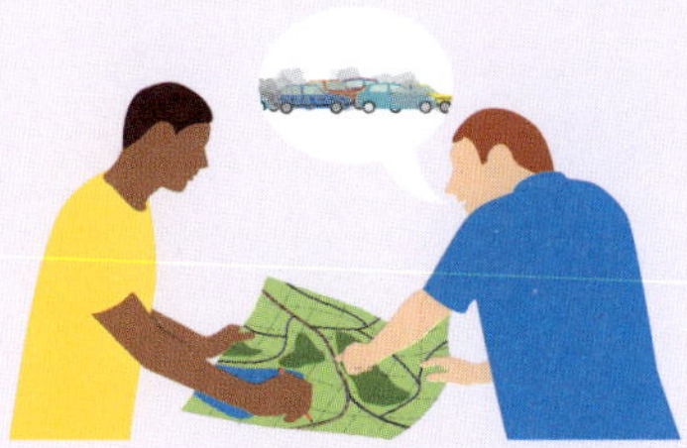

Allow for traffic delays when estimating how long it'll take.

allow for
take something into consideration before making a plan

You need to think ahead and save some money for the future.

think ahead
think about the future and plan for it

The two directors had several meetings to firm up the details of the new contract.

firm up
make something more definite

We've been meaning to get a new kitchen for years, but we never get around to it.

get around to
find the time to do something

Look ahead and picture what you want to be doing in five years' time.

look ahead
think about what might happen in the future

The store weaseled out of giving us a refund by claiming we had broken the vase.

weasel out of
avoid doing something you had agreed to do in a sneaky way (informal)

Seb said he'd help me paint the house, but he went back on his promise.

go back on
fail to keep a promise or agreement

Cleo didn't want to go out, so she pretended to be sick to get out of it.

get out of
avoid doing something you had agreed to do

Aa 17.3 MATCH UP THE PAIRS OF SENTENCES THAT MEAN THE SAME THING

Seb said he'd help me paint the house, but he went back on his promise. → Seb said he'd help me paint the house, but he did not keep his promise.

1. Allow for traffic delays when estimating how long the journey will take.
2. We've been meaning to get a new kitchen for years, but we never get around to it.
3. Giovanni forgot about the art project, but he managed to throw something together.
4. The two directors had several meetings to firm up the details of the new contract.
5. I asked Sabrina if she wanted to go camping, but she threw out the idea.
6. The negotiating teams stayed up until after midnight hammering out a new treaty.

- The two directors had several meetings to make the new contract more definite.
- Seb said he'd help me paint the house, but he did not keep his promise.
- I asked Sabrina if she wanted to go camping, but she rejected the idea.
- We've been meaning to get a new kitchen for years, but haven't found the time for it.
- Take traffic delays into consideration when estimating how long the journey will take.
- The negotiating teams stayed up to discuss and reach an agreement on a new treaty.
- Giovanni forgot about the art project, but he managed to do it without preparation.

Aa 17.4 FILL IN THE GAPS USING THE PHRASAL VERBS IN THE PANEL

We want to get married, but we haven't *pinned down* a location yet.

1. They stayed up until after midnight ____________ a new treaty.

2. Cleo pretended to be sick to ____________ going out.

3. Dexter was going to ask Becky out, but he ____________.

4. You need to ____________ and save money for the future.

hammering out
think ahead
~~pinned down~~
get out of
chickened out

17.5 LOOK AT THE PICTURES AND COMPLETE THE SENTENCES USING PHRASAL VERBS

Kwang had been planning to study medicine, but *ended up* studying French.

3 ____________ and picture what you want to be doing in five years' time.

1 You should ____________ before setting off on a long car journey.

4 The store ____________ giving us a refund by claiming we had broken the vase.

2 Seb said he'd help me paint the house, but he ____________ his promise.

5 Ed had promised to do a bungee jump with me, but ____________ at the last minute.

17.6 LISTEN TO THE AUDIO, THEN NUMBER THE SENTENCES IN THE ORDER YOU HEAR THEM

A My dad wanted to buy a motorcycle for ages, but I never expected him to go through with it. ☐

B We want to get married in summer, but we haven't pinned down a location yet. ☐

C I asked Sabrina if she wanted to go camping, but she threw out the idea. [1]

D We've been meaning to get a new kitchen for years, but we never get around to it. ☐

E Kwang had been planning to study medicine, but ended up studying French. ☐

F Seb said he'd help me paint the house, but he went back on his promise. ☐

G Giovanni forgot about the art project, but he managed to throw something together. ☐

18 The senses

18.1 HEARING

Listen up! You're going to fail your exam unless you start working a bit harder.

listen up
pay attention

Andy hid behind the curtain so he could **listen in on** Carmen and Simon's conversation.

listen in (on)
secretly listen to someone

Dayita **listened to** the radio while she ate her breakfast.

listen to
pay attention to someone talking or something making a sound

Marion asked her son to **listen out for** the doorbell while she was in the garden.

listen out for
listen attentively to hear a noise you are expecting

Have you **heard about** the new gym in town? It's supposed to be great.

hear about
receive information about something

Please **hear** me **out**! I don't want to be a lawyer. I want to be an actor!

hear out
listen to someone without interrupting

18.2 SMELL AND TASTE

Alex's cookies **smelled of** cinnamon. I asked to try one.

smell of
have the smell of something

Whatever Pablo has cooked is **stinking** the whole house **out**.

stink out
cause somewhere to smell unpleasant (informal)

That journalist's been **sniffing around** again trying to find out what's going on.

sniff around
try to find information

This soup is delicious! It **tastes of** tomato and basil.

taste of
have the flavor of something

See also:
look into **20**

18.3 SIGHT

Robert has been looking for his glasses all afternoon. He can't find them anywhere.

look for
search for something

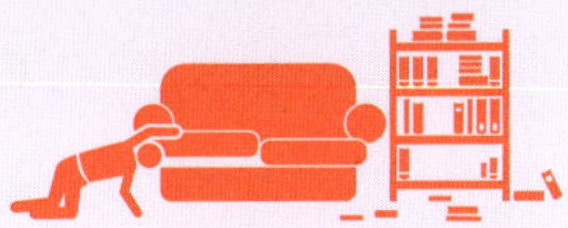

The geologist looked at each of the rocks. They were unlike anything he'd seen before.

look at
examine something

We all looked on in silence as the magician seemed to cut the person in half.

look on
watch something without taking part

While you're in the national park, look out for bald eagles near the rivers and lakes.

look out for
pay attention to notice something

The children looked over the wall, trying to see where the ball had landed.

look over
raise yourself to see past an obstacle

The scary scene in the movie made everyone look away.

look away
turn your eyes away from something

Sarah and Dionne looked into the well. There was no sign of the bottom.

look into
look at a hole, room, or hollow object to see what is inside

Marcus looked through his telescope to see the moon.

look through
look at one side of something to see what is on the other side

Vineeta's summer house has the perfect location. It looks out over a lake.

look out over
have a view of

Fiona spied on her colleagues to steal their ideas.

spy on
secretly watch someone

Aa 18.4 READ THE STATEMENTS AND MARK THE CORRECT MEANING

Fiona spied on her colleagues.
Fiona is a spy. ☐
Fiona secretly watched her colleagues. ☑
Fiona thinks her colleagues are spies. ☐

1 The soup tastes of tomato and basil.
The soup has only tomato and basil in it. ☐
The soup has a tomato and basil flavor. ☐
The soup is missing tomato and basil. ☐

2 Marcus looked through his telescope.
Marcus bought a telescope. ☐
Marcus saw a telescope. ☐
Marcus used his telescope. ☐

3 Robert looked for his glasses.
Robert wanted his glasses back. ☐
Robert searched for his glasses. ☐
Robert bought new glasses. ☐

4 Please hear me out!
Please listen to me! ☐
Please come outside! ☐
Please leave me alone! ☐

18.5 LISTEN TO THE AUDIO AND MATCH THE IMAGES TO THE CORRECT PHRASAL VERBS

1 

2 

3 

4 

5 

6 

- look at
- taste of
- listen in on
- sniff around
- look through
- listen out for
- stink out

Aa 18.6 WRITE THE CORRECT PHRASAL VERB NEXT TO ITS DEFINITION, FILLING IN THE MISSING LETTERS

watch something without taking part = l o o k o n

1 try to find information about someone or something = s _ _ _ _ a _ _ _ _ _
2 examine something = l _ _ _ a _
3 have a view of = l _ _ _ o _ _ o _ _ _
4 turn your eyes away from something = l _ _ _ a _ _ _

Aa 18.7 MATCH THE DEFINITIONS TO THE CORRECT PHRASAL VERBS

raise yourself to see past an obstacle → look over

1. secretly listen to someone
2. cause somewhere to smell unpleasant
3. pay attention to notice something
4. receive information about something
5. pay attention
6. listen to someone without interrupting
7. watch something without taking part

- hear out
- listen up
- look over
- stink out
- look out for
- look on
- hear about
- listen in (on)

Aa 18.8 FILL IN THE GAPS USING THE PHRASAL VERBS IN THE PANEL

The scary scene in the movie made everyone *look away*. 

1. Alex's cookies ________________ cinnamon. I asked to try one. 
2. Have you ________________ the new gym in town? It's supposed to be great. 
3. Dayita ________________ the radio while she ate her breakfast. 
4. Fiona ________________ her colleagues to steal their ideas. 
5. Sarah and Dionne ________________ the well. There was no sign of the bottom. 

- smelled of
- spied on
- ~~look away~~
- looked into
- listened to
- heard about

19 Movement and progress

19.1 MOVEMENT AND PROGRESS

Martin was exhausted, and began to fall behind the other runners.

fall behind
move more slowly than the people around you

The rain made it hard for the hikers to keep going, but they pressed on.

press on
continue despite difficulties

Tanya turned away as the nurse gave her the injection.

turn away
turn your head or body so that you are no longer facing something

The security guards told us to stop taking photos of the building and move along.

move along
leave a certain place (usually said by someone in authority)

As the train went through the mountain range, Ted took some photographs.

go through
move through a room or space

There was a loud knock at the door. Hassan stood up and went to answer it.

stand up
rise from a seated position

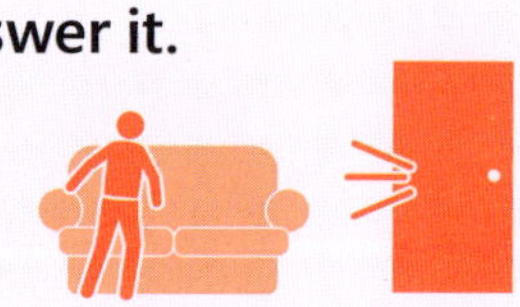

The saleswoman came up to Fabio and asked if he needed any help.

come up to
approach someone, come close to someone

As we came down from the summit, the weather became much worse.

come down (from)
move toward the ground or bottom of something

The monkey climbed up the tree with Kazuo's camera.

climb up
move toward the top of something (often using your arms as well as legs)

Kazuo got the monkey to climb down by offering it a banana.

climb down
move toward the bottom of something (often using your arms as well as legs)

See also:
climb down **44** fall behind **20** get down **46**, **53**
go through **54** turn around **33** turn away **5**

Terry doubled back when he realized he'd walked past the entrance to the gallery.

double back
turn around and go in the direction you just came from

When I heard someone calling my name, I turned around.

turn around
turn yourself so that you face the opposite direction

Clive lifted his daughter up so that she could see the deer.

lift up
raise someone or something

Doug dropped back to help one of the other hikers, who had injured himself.

drop back
start to move more slowly than others

Helen told her son to get down from the garden wall.

get down (from)
move to the ground or a lower position

19.2 PHRASAL VERBS WITH "WALK"

The visitors walked around the palace gardens.

walk around
move around a place on foot

The explorers walked into the cave.

walk in(to)
enter a room, building, or enclosed space on foot

A line of tourists slowly walked over the ancient bridge.

walk over
move over an object on foot

While we were chatting, Mani walked off without saying where he was going.

walk off
leave on foot (often without an explanation)

Janine grabbed her coat and walked out of the room.

walk out (of)
leave a room, building, or enclosed space on foot

19.3 LISTEN TO THE AUDIO, THEN NUMBER THE SENTENCES IN THE ORDER YOU HEAR THEM

A  While we were chatting, Mani walked off without saying where he was going. ☐

B  Terry doubled back when he realized he'd walked past the entrance to the gallery. ☐

C  There was a loud knock at the door. Hassan stood up and went to answer it. [1]

D  The rain made it hard for the hikers to keep going, but they pressed on. ☐

E  The security guards told us to stop taking photos of the building and move along. ☐

19.4 MATCH THE BEGINNINGS OF THE SENTENCES TO THE CORRECT ENDINGS

Janine grabbed her coat → and walked out of the room.

1. Kazuo got the monkey to climb
2. The explorers walked
3. Doug dropped back to help one of
4. As we came down from the summit,
5. The saleswoman came up
6. Clive lifted his daughter up

- down by offering it a banana.
- into the cave.
- and walked out of the room.
- so that she could see the deer.
- the other hikers, who had injured himself.
- the weather became much worse.
- to Fabio and asked if he needed any help.

Aa 19.5 CROSS OUT THE INCORRECT WORDS IN EACH SENTENCE

A line of tourists slowly walked ~~around~~ / over / ~~through~~ the ancient bridge.

1 When I heard someone calling my name, I turned about / around / off.

2  Martin was exhausted, and began to fall / run / jump behind the other runners.

3  Clive lifted his daughter over / down / up so that she could see the deer.

4  Janine grabbed her coat and walked back / out / down of the room.

5  Doug dropped out / in / back to help one of the other hikers, who had injured himself.

Aa 19.6 FILL IN THE GAPS, PUTTING THE WORDS IN THE CORRECT ORDER

[the] [walked] [around]

The visitors *walked* *around* *the* palace gardens.

[away] [as] [turned]

1 Tanya _____ _____ _____ the nurse gave her the injection.

[climbed] [the] [up]

2 The monkey _____ _____ _____ tree with Kazuo's camera.

[get] [from] [down]

3 Helen told her son to _____ _____ _____ the garden wall.

[the] [through] [went]

4 As the train _____ _____ _____ mountain range, Ted took some photographs.

20 Studying and research

20.1 STUDY AND RESEARCH

I'm moving to Tokyo for a year. I need to brush up on my Japanese.

brush up on
practice, revise

Nadia stayed up all night trying to work out the answer to the equation.

work out
solve a problem

The library was full of students swotting up on English grammar.

swot up on (UK)
(informal) study a subject

I kept making mistakes trying to answer the question, so decided to start over.

start over (US)
start something again

Fiona worked through the problems in her code to fix the issues.

work through
deal with a problem carefully and methodically

Sam has dived into his new project. He spent all weekend working on it.

dive in(to)
start doing something with enthusiasm

Patsy's research focuses on space travel.

focus on
give attention to

She's looking into how astronauts might travel to Mars one day.

look into
investigate, research, or find out about something

20.2 MAKING A PRESENTATION

At the start of your presentation, lay out the main points you are going to discuss.

lay out
present or explain in a clear way

After introducing your topic, you should then move on to presenting each of your arguments.

move on (to)
proceed to the next point

See also:
fall behind **20** keep up with **33** look into **20**
move on **45** work out **26**, **33** work through **45**

Hi, Arjun. Do you know what "burdensome" means?

No, I don't. You'll have to **look** it **up** in a dictionary.

look up
find information online or in a reference book

The practical assessment and the written exam both **count toward** your final grade.

count toward
contribute toward

Bill is trying to **cram in** as much studying as possible before the exam.

cram in (UK)
fit a lot of something into a small space or a short period of time

Emma was sick for most of the spring. She has **fallen behind** the other students in her year.

fall behind
not keep up with

Even though Leo is the youngest in his class, he manages to **keep up with** the other children.

keep up with
improve at the same speed as someone

Noah is **majoring in** international politics at college. He hopes to become an ambassador one day.

major in (US)
study something as your main subject at university

Please take care writing your presentation. You'll be **marked down** for incorrect spelling.

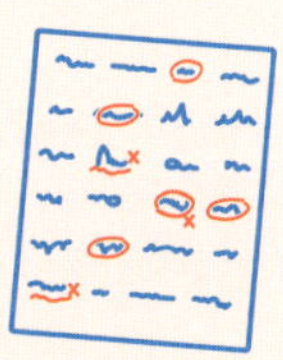

mark down
give someone a lower grade

At the end of your presentation, you should **sum up** each of your conclusions.

sum up
give a summary of your argument in the conclusion

Aa 20.3 MARK THE SENTENCES THAT ARE CORRECT

I'm moving to Tokyo for a year. I need to brush up on my Japanese. ☑

I'm moving to Tokyo for a year. I need to brush down my Japanese. ☐

1 

Leo is the youngest in his class, but manages to keep up with his classmates. ☐

Leo is the youngest in his class, but manages to keep on at his classmates. ☐

2 

She's looking into how astronauts might travel to Mars one day. ☐

She's looking onto how astronauts might travel to Mars one day. ☐

3 

Sam has dived off his new project. He spent all weekend working on it. ☐

Sam has dived into his new project. He spent all weekend working on it. ☐

4 

The library was full of students swotting up on English grammar. ☐

The library was full of students swotting out on English grammar. ☐

5 

At the start of your presentation, lay out the main points you are going to discuss. ☐

At the start of your presentation, lay on the main points you are going to discuss. ☐

Aa 20.4 FILL IN THE GAPS, PUTTING THE WORDS IN THE CORRECT ORDER

the | work | out

Nadia stayed up all night trying to *work* *out* *the* answer to the equation.

in | majoring | is

1 Noah _____ _____ _____ international politics at college.

start | to | over

2 I kept making mistakes, so I decided _____ _____ _____ .

space | focuses | on

3 Patsy's research _____ _____ _____ travel.

through | the | worked

4 Fiona _____ _____ _____ problems in her code to fix the issues.

Aa 20.5 READ THE ARTICLE AND WRITE THE PHRASAL VERBS ABOVE THEIR DEFINITIONS

How to structure a presentation: At the start of your presentation, **lay out** the main points you are going to discuss. Then, **move on to** presenting each of your arguments clearly and succinctly. **Focus on** being coherent and logical as you speak, making sure to emphasize all important points. At the end of your presentation, you should finish by **summing up** each of your conclusions. Include time for interaction with the audience and **work through** all questions calmly and confidently. Take care when writing your presentation, as you will be **marked down** for incorrect spelling and this will **count toward** your final assessment.

sum up — sum up your argument

1. ________ deal with a problem methodically
2. ________ proceed to the next point
3. ________ contribute toward
4. ________ give someone a lower grade
5. ________ give attention to
6. ________ present in a clear way

20.6 LISTEN TO THE AUDIO, THEN NUMBER THE PICTURES IN THE ORDER YOU HEAR THEM

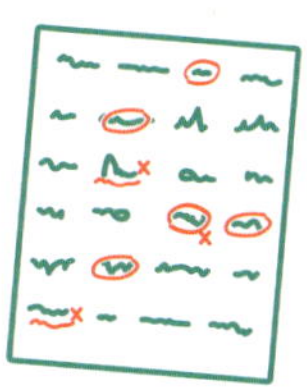

A ☐

B 1

C ☐

D ☐

E ☐

F ☐

G ☐

H ☐

21 At school

21.1 SCHOOL

Ola dropped out of high school without any qualifications, but she went on to become a successful businesswoman.

drop out
leave school or university without finishing your studies

Miguel handed in his assignment five minutes before the deadline.

hand in (to)
give a piece of work to a teacher, give something to someone in authority

The teacher handed out the worksheet to each member of the class.

hand out (to)
give something to each member of a group, distribute

The teacher wiped the notes off the board before Ed had finished copying them.

wipe off
remove something (with a cloth)

Schools break up in July in the UK. There is a six-week summer holiday.

break up (UK)
close for the holidays

Ramu's working on a new art project. It's a huge painting of New York.

work on
spend time or put effort into something

When the class finished, Arun packed up his things and got ready to leave.

pack up
gather your things and put them in a bag or box

Good morning class.
Please take out your books.

Now turn to page 25 and complete the exercises.

take out
remove something (from a bag)

turn to
open a book at a specific page

See also:
break up **3**, **15**, **29**, **38** mess around **41**
take out **3**, **14**, **28** turn to **13**, **45**, **50** wipe off **14**

21.2 BAD BEHAVIOR

You've spent too much time goofing off this semester, Jesse.

I will not stand for laziness. It's time you started working harder.

goof off (US)
waste time, avoid doing work

not stand for
not tolerate, not allow someone to do something

The kids have been playing up all morning.

play up (UK)
be naughty, misbehave

Ffion is so naughty. She's always fooling around in class instead of paying attention.

fool around
behave in a silly way

Despite the teacher's warnings, the children carried on misbehaving.

carry on
continue (doing something)

The teacher told his students to stop messing around, and to do their work.

mess around
misbehave, do something other than what you should be doing

Mateo and Juanita are very naughty, but Martina lets them get away with it.

get away with
do something wrong without being punished for it

Rosie is very rude to her teachers. She's always answering back.

answer back
respond rudely (usually to a teacher or parent)

Marco was furious about the broken window, but he let Gio and Carmen off with a warning.

let off (with)
not punish someone, or give them a very light punishment

Zosia told the children off when she saw the terrible mess they had made.

tell off
reprimand someone when they have done something wrong

Aa 21.3 READ THE STATEMENTS AND MARK THE CORRECT MEANING

Ramu's working on a new art project.
Ramu's thinking of a new art project. ☐
Ramu's spending time on a new art project. ☑
Ramu's interested in a new art project. ☐

1 Schools break up in July in the UK.
Schools open in July. ☐
Schools organize events in July. ☐
Schools close in July. ☐

2 Marco let Gio and Carmen off with a warning.
Marco punished Gio and Carmen. ☐
Marco did not punish Gio and Carmen. ☐
Marco chatted with Gio and Carmen. ☐

3 Zosia told the children off for the mess they had made.
Zosia congratulated the children. ☐
Zosia reprimanded the children. ☐
Zosia helped the children clean up. ☐

4 Rosie is always answering back to her teachers.
Rosie responds rudely to her teachers. ☐
Rosie responds politely to her teachers. ☐
Rosie does not respond to her teachers. ☐

Aa 21.4 MATCH THE PICTURES TO THE CORRECT SENTENCES

Miguel handed in his assignment just before the deadline.

1 

Rosie is very rude. She's always answering back.

2 

The teacher handed out the worksheet to each student.

3 

After the class, Arun packed up his things and got ready to leave.

4 

Ramu's working on a huge painting of New York.

21.5 LISTEN TO THE AUDIO AND MARK THE PHRASAL VERBS YOU HEAR

tell off	☑	play up	☐	drop out	☐
1 tell off	☐	not stand for	☐	get away with	☐
2 hand in	☐	drop out	☐	take out	☐
3 carry on	☐	answer back	☐	drop out	☐
4 tell off	☐	take out	☐	play up	☐

Aa 21.6 WRITE THE CORRECT PHRASAL VERB NEXT TO ITS DEFINITION

close for the holidays = *break up*

1. give something to each member of a group = ____________
2. remove something (with a cloth) = ____________
3. not tolerate, not allow someone to do something = ____________
4. leave school without finishing your studies = ____________
5. look for a certain page = ____________

Aa 21.7 LOOK AT THE PICTURES AND COMPLETE THE SENTENCES USING THE PHRASAL VERBS IN THE PANEL

Ola *dropped out* of school, but went on to become a successful businesswoman.

1. Good morning class. Please ____________ your books.

2. The kids have been ____________ all morning.

3. Despite the teacher's warnings, the children ____________ misbehaving.

4. You've spent too much time ____________ this semester, Jesse.

5. Mateo and Juanita are very naughty, but Martina lets them ____________ it.

playing up | take out | goofing off | get away with | carried on | ~~dropped out~~

22 At work

22.1 STARTING AND FINISHING

I clock in at 9am every morning.

clock in
start work

I clock off at 5pm every afternoon.

clock off
finish work

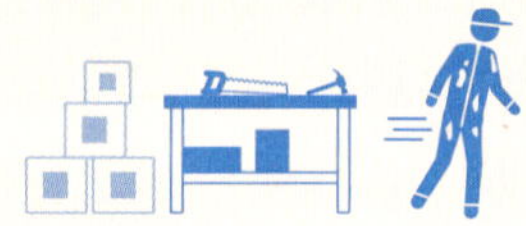

Despite the storm, the engineers soldiered on and installed the new phone line.

soldier on
continue trying to achieve something despite difficulties

Debbie took the afternoon off so she could go to the dentist.

take off
take a break from work for a certain amount of time

I'm not feeling very well today, so I'm going to call in sick.

call in
telephone your workplace

Steve gets off work early on Fridays so he can collect his children from school.

get off
finish work

22.2 MEETINGS

Our manager was busy, so she had to call off our meeting.

call off
cancel an event

Let's talk over all your designs and make a decision.

talk over
discuss

Angela meets up with her colleagues once a week to discuss all their new ideas.

meet up (with)
get together with

I might be busy tomorrow, but let's pencil in a meeting anyway.

pencil in
agree a time or date that might be changed later

See also:
call in **4**, **50** get off **9**
take off **5**, **6**, **9**, **55** talk over **36**

22.3 WORKING

The applications for the new manager position are piling up. I'd better start looking through them.

pile up
increase to an unmanageable amount

Fiona was struggling to finalize the company's accounts, but she kept plugging away at them.

plug away (at)
work hard to achieve something difficult

Jennie's been slogging away trying to finish writing her presentation.

slog away (at)
work very hard for a long time

Kamal's manager chased up the report, which was already a week late.

chase up
ask someone for something (again)

Ted used to be very proactive, but he's been slacking off lately.

slack off
avoid hard work

Ola is carrying out a survey about worker satisfaction.

carry out
complete a task

Gio has been on vacation for two weeks, so he has a lot of work to catch up on.

catch up on
do work that you did not have time to do earlier

I've got lots to do! I need to knuckle down and get it finished.

knuckle down
start to work very hard

I've been very busy lately, but I have next week off work.

have off
have a break from work for a certain amount of time

Aa 22.4 LOOK AT THE PICTURES AND COMPLETE THE SENTENCES USING THE PHRASAL VERBS IN THE PANEL

Steve ___*gets off*___ work early on Fridays so he can collect his children from school.

4. Our manager was busy, so she had to ____________________ our meeting.

1. Ted used to be very proactive, but he's been ____________________ lately.

5. Jennie's been ____________________ trying to finish writing her presentation.

2. I've got lots to do! I need to ____________________ and get it finished.

6. Kamal's manager ____________________ the report, which was already a week late.

3. Angela ____________________ her colleagues once a week to discuss all their new ideas.

7. I ____________________ at 9am every morning.

call off	chased up	~~gets off~~	slacking off	clock in
knuckle down	meets up with	slogging away		

22.5 LISTEN TO THE AUDIO AND MARK THE PHRASAL VERBS YOU HEAR

- A call in ☐
- B knuckle down ☐
- C slog away at ☑
- D have off ☐
- E call off ☐
- F chase up ☐
- G meet up with ☐
- H carry out ☐
- I talk over ☐

22.6 MATCH THE PICTURES TO THE CORRECT SENTENCES

→ Let's talk over all your designs and make a decision.

1 

2 

3 

4 

I clock off at 5pm every afternoon.

Let's talk over all your designs and make a decision.

Ola is carrying out a survey about worker satisfaction.

I've been very busy lately, but I have next week off work.

I'm not feeling very well today, so I'm going to call in sick.

22.7 REWRITE THE SENTENCES, CORRECTING THE ERRORS

Gio has been on vacation for two weeks, so he has a lot of work to **throw up on**.
Gio has been on vacation for two weeks, so he has a lot of work to catch up on.

1. The applications for the new manager position are **piling over**. I'd better start looking through them.

2. Fiona was struggling to finalize the company's accounts, but she kept **switching away** at them.

3. Debbie **took** the afternoon **down** so she could go to the dentist.

4. Despite the storm, the engineers **marched on** and installed the new phone line.

23 Careers

23.1 CAREERS

After 35 years running his own company, Robert is **standing down** and retiring.

stand down
leave an important job or position

His daughter Jess is **taking over** the family business.

take over
take responsibility for a company or role

Katie has been a therapist for 20 years, so she has a lot of experience to **draw on**.

draw on
make use of your experience

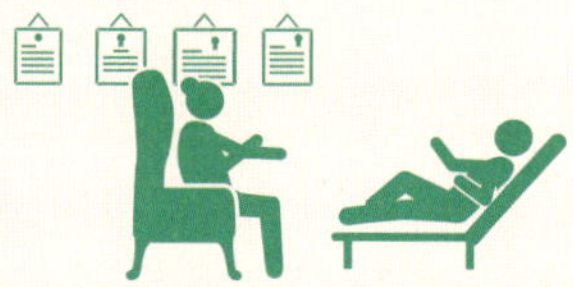

Olivia is trying to **get into** journalism. She's just started an internship at a radio station.

get into
become involved in something, start a career

If I ever lose my job at the bank, I'll always have my cooking skills to **fall back on**.

fall back on
use skills that you already have (when things go wrong)

When he left school, Paul **set out** to become a millionaire by the time he reached 30.

set out
begin doing something with a specific aim in mind

Carolina went on a training course to help her **get ahead at** work.

get ahead (at)
improve your position at work

I **went back to** my job as a mechanic when my children started school.

go back to
return to a job after a break

Joanna is **winding down** her business to take a job managing a large hotel.

wind down
gradually bring to an end

Chad just finished his degree and is **applying for** jobs in the media.

applying for
ask to be considered for a job

See also:
get into **31** put off **55** set out **35**, **53**
wind down **31**

Thanks to his impressive portfolio, Elliot walked into a job with a leading fashion designer.

walk into
find a job easily

Marvin has become such a successful tennis player that he's branching out into coaching younger players.

branch out (into)
start doing something different (but related)

Ken's going to burn himself out if he keeps working 16 hours a day.

burn out
become exhausted by working too much

We have chosen Diana to head up our new sales department.

head up
lead, be in charge of a department or organization

I thought I wanted to be a lawyer, but the workload put me off.

put off
make someone dislike a person or thing

Femi has thrown himself into his new job at the hair salon. He loves it!

throw (oneself) into
begin doing something with great enthusiasm

Naina is planning to go into teaching when she finishes university.

go into
start a career in something

Even though he doesn't like his job, Tom is sticking with it until he gets promoted.

stick with
continue despite difficulties

Brian has started selling umbrellas in his store to cash in on the recent terrible weather.

cash in on
take advantage of a situation to make money

23.2 LISTEN TO THE AUDIO AND MATCH THE IMAGES TO THE CORRECT PHRASAL VERBS

1

2

3

4

go back to | stick with | head up

wind down | draw on

23.3 READ THE STATEMENTS AND MARK THE CORRECT MEANING

Femi has thrown himself into his new job.
Femi is anxious about his new job. ☐
Femi is enthusiastic about his new job. ☑
Femi doesn't like his new job. ☐

1 Elliot walked into a job with a fashion designer.
Elliot walks to work. ☐
Elliot found the job easily. ☐
Elliot was late to work. ☐

2 Katie has a lot of experience to draw on.
Katie is an artist. ☐
Katie makes use of her experience. ☐
Katie wants to build experience. ☐

3 Naina is planning to go into teaching.
Naina is planning to meet her teacher. ☐
Naina is planning to become a teacher. ☐
Naina is planning to go to school. ☐

4 I went back to my job as a mechanic.
I went to meet the mechanic. ☐
I went back to work. ☐
I want to become a mechanic. ☐

5 Diana heads up our new sales department.
Diana leads the new department. ☐
Diana founded the new department. ☐
Diana dislikes the new department. ☐

6 Chad is applying for jobs in the media.
Chad is not looking for jobs. ☐
Chad is employed in the media. ☐
Chad is looking for jobs in the media. ☐

7 Olivia is trying to get into journalism.
Olivia is trying to become a journalist. ☐
Olivia is trying to meet a journalist. ☐
Olivia is a journalist. ☐

Aa 23.4 WRITE THE CORRECT PHRASAL VERB NEXT TO ITS DEFINITION, FILLING IN THE MISSING LETTERS

leave an important job or position = s t a n d d o w n

1. continue despite difficulties = s _ _ _ _ w _ _ _
2. ask to be considered for a job = a _ _ _ _ f _ _
3. take responsibility for a company or role = t _ _ _ o _ _ _
4. return to a job after a break = g _ b _ _ _ t _
5. gradually bring to an end = w _ _ _ d _ _ _

Aa 23.5 WRITE THE PHRASAL VERBS FROM THE PANEL UNDER THE CORRECT DEFINITIONS

improve your position at work

get ahead (at)

1. become involved in something, start a career

____

2. become exhausted by working too much

____

3. start doing something different (but related)

____

4. make someone dislike a person or thing

____

5. take advantage of a situation to make money

____

6. use skills that you already have when things go wrong

____

7. begin doing something with a specific aim in mind

____

cash in on | set out | branch out (into) | put off | burn out | get into | ~~get ahead (at)~~ | fall back on

24 Business

24.1 BUSINESS

We are proud to announce that our two banks are entering into a partnership.

enter into
begin a (business) relationship

Katie's trying to drum up interest in her café by offering free samples of her cakes.

drum up
increase support for something

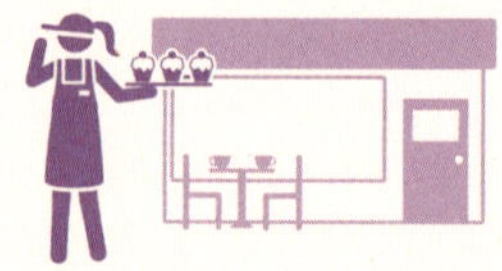

Marco's garden center is doing well. It turns over almost $250,000 a year.

turn over
(about a business) earn an amount of money over a certain period of time

Alan's sportswear company profited from the cold weather earlier this year.

profit from
gain a benefit from a situation

The board has finally come to a decision about the new logo for the company.

come to
arrive at, reach (a decision)

Chrissie has just started up her own hair salon. It opened last week.

start up
open a business

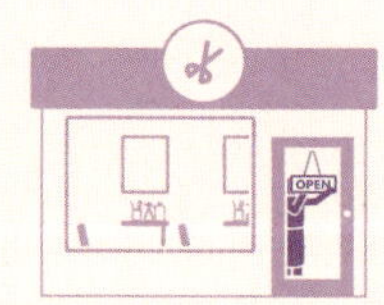

Mario's gas station has just gone under. It had been struggling for a long time.

go under
go bankrupt

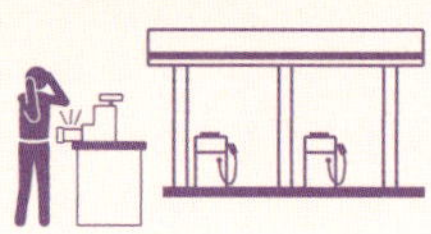

Ellie's company deals in antiques. She sells pieces from all over the world.

deal in
buy and sell goods

Elsa's tired of running her own business. She's decided to sell up.

sell up
sell a business

The bank agreed to write off the debt, saving Ethan's company from bankruptcy.

write off
cancel a debt

See also:
come to **14** open up **45**

All of the banks in our town have closed down. Everyone's using online banking.

close down
close permanently

My plans to expand my business fell through when the bank refused to lend me enough money.

fall through
fail to happen

Gemma has bought out all the other partners. She now owns the whole company.

buy out
buy someone's share of a business

Rita's company sells furniture, but farms out all of its manufacturing to other people.

farm out (to)
give some of your work to people who do not work for your company

Our business is growing, so we are taking on more staff.

take on
employ

We need the CEO to sign off on this important decision.

sign off on
give official approval to something

A new bookstore is opening up in our neighborhood.

open up
open for the first time

Al's store is selling off a lot of its stock. There are some great bargains there.

sell off
sell something quickly at a reduced price

The company is facing difficulties. We may need to lay off some staff.

lay off
stop employing someone

Could you draw up a contract for our new clients?

draw up
write a contract

Aa 24.2 MATCH THE PICTURES TO THE CORRECT SENTENCES

1 

2 

3 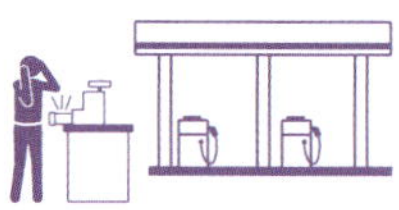

4 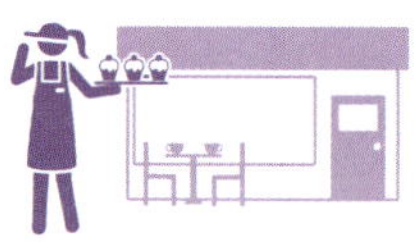

We are proud to announce that our two banks are entering into a partnership.

All of the banks in our town have closed down. Everyone's using online banking.

Mario's gas station has just gone under. It had been struggling for a long time.

Katie's trying to drum up interest in her café by offering free samples of her cakes.

The bank agreed to write off the debt, saving Ethan's company from bankruptcy.

Aa 24.3 CROSS OUT THE INCORRECT WORDS IN EACH SENTENCE

Elsa's tired of running her own business. She's decided to ~~trade~~ / sell / ~~walk~~ up.

1 Marco's garden center is doing well. It turns down / over / forward almost $250,000 a year.

2 We need the CEO to sign / mark / stamp off on this important decision.

3 The board has finally arrived / reached / come to a decision about the new logo for the company.

4 Ellie's company deals on / in / for antiques. She sells pieces from all over the world.

5 Could you sketch / draw / paint up a contract for our new clients?

6 The company is facing difficulties. We may need to lay off / out / down some staff.

24.4 LISTEN TO THE AUDIO AND MARK THE PHRASAL VERBS YOU HEAR

write off	☑	sell off	☐	take on	☐
1 close down	☐	fall through	☐	start up	☐
2 gone under	☐	buy out	☐	come to	☐
3 sign off	☐	draw up	☐	lay off	☐
4 take on	☐	open up	☐	drum up	☐
5 enter into	☐	fall through	☐	fall from	☐
6 walk up	☐	farm out to	☐	profit from	☐

24.5 FILL IN THE GAPS USING THE PHRASAL VERBS IN THE PANEL

Could you draw up a contract for our new clients?

1 Our business is growing, so we are ______ more staff.

2 A new bookstore is ______ in our neighborhood.

3 Chrissie has just ______ her own hair salon. It opened last week.

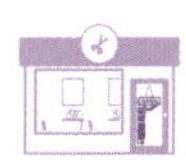

4 Gemma has ______ all the other partners.

5 Al's store is ______ a lot of its stock.

6 Alan's sportswear company ______ the cold weather.

- opening up
- bought out
- selling off
- taking on
- ~~draw up~~
- profited from
- started up

25 Numbers and amounts

25.1 NUMBERS AND AMOUNTS

Katie's bills have been stacking up. She's in a lot of debt now.

stack up
increase in number or amount

The temperature varies a bit in the summer, but it averages out at about 25°C.

average out (at)
result in an average of

The price for our cruise was going to be $1,207, but the travel agent agreed to round it down to $1,200.

round down (to)
reduce a number to a nearby number (usually ending in zero)

We estimated the cost of the project to be £14,900, but rounded it up to the nearest thousand.

round up (to)
increase a number to a nearby number (usually ending in zero)

The kids are counting down the days before we go camping.

count down
count the amount of time before something happens

Alfie counted out the money he owed me and placed it on the table.

count out
count things one by one and place them somewhere

The company's share price has been falling, but it's finally starting to bottom out.

bottom out
stop getting worse, reach its lowest point

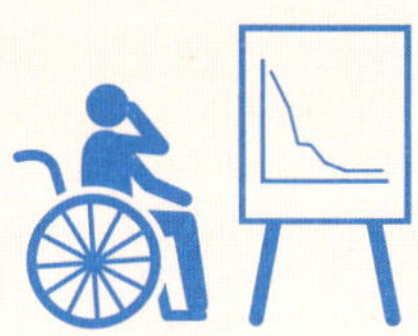

After falling dramatically in May, the price of gold has evened out over the past two months.

even out
become level, contain fewer differences or irregularities

The number of people buying clothes online shot up last year.

shoot up
increase dramatically

Over the last six months, it has started to level out.

level out
become level, stop increasing or decreasing

See also:
add up **14**, **41** take away **30**, **55**

The coach divided the children up into two equal teams.

divide up (into)
separate into groups, pieces, or sections

If you want to set yourself a budget, start by adding up all your monthly expenses.

add up
calculate the total

Renovating a house is very expensive. The cost soon mounts up.

mount up
gradually increase in number or amount

Shreya counted up the number of people wanting coffee and went to make some.

count up
add together things or people belonging to a group

When Georgia was paying her check, she added on a 20% tip.

add on
attach an extra thing or amount to something

25.2 CALCULATIONS

If you add 20 and 4 together, you get 24.

add together
calculate the total of two or more numbers

The teacher asked what's left when you take 4 away from 20.

take away (from)
subtract

For the next question, the class had to multiply 20 by 4.

multiply by
add a number to itself a certain number of times

Does anyone know what 20 divided by 4 equals?

divide by
find how many times a larger number contains a smaller number

Aa 25.3 MARK THE SENTENCES THAT ARE CORRECT

The kids are counting down the days before we go camping. ☑
The kids are counting below the days before we go camping. ☐

1. The number of people buying clothes online shot up last year. ☐
   The number of people buying clothes online bought up last year. ☐

2. The coach divided the children above into two equal teams. ☐
   The coach divided the children up into two equal teams. ☐

3. Shreya counted up the number of people wanting coffee and went to make some. ☐
   Shreya counted on the number of people wanting coffee and went to make some. ☐

4. When Georgia was paying her check, she added on a 20% tip. ☐
   When Georgia was paying her check, she divided on a 20% tip. ☐

25.4 LISTEN TO THE AUDIO, THEN NUMBER THE PICTURES IN THE ORDER YOU HEAR THEM

A ☐

B 1

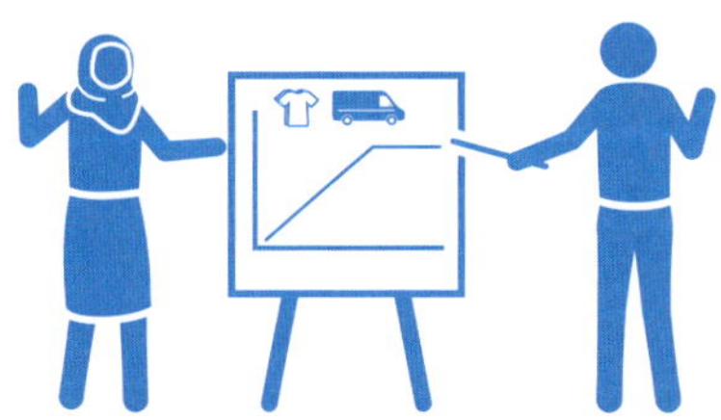

C ☐

D ☐

E ☐

F ☐

Aa 25.5 REWRITE THE SENTENCES, CORRECTING THE ERRORS

Alfie **counted of** the money he owed me and placed it on the table.

Alfie counted out the money he owed me and placed it on the table.

1. Katie's bills have been **stacking over**. She's in a lot of debt now.

____

2. The company's share price has been falling, but it's finally starting to **ground out**.

____

3. The temperature varies a bit in the summer, but it **averages in at** about 25°C.

____

4. We estimated the cost of the project to be £14,900, but **mounted** it **up to** the nearest thousand.

____

5. If you want to set yourself a budget, start by **scoring up** all your monthly expenses.

____

Aa 25.6 WRITE THE CORRECT PHRASAL VERB NEXT TO ITS DEFINITION

gradually increase in number or amount = *mount up*

1. count the amount of time before something happens = ______________
2. calculate the total = ______________
3. result in an average of = ______________
4. become level, stop increasing or decreasing = ______________
5. count things one by one and place them somewhere = ______________
6. stop getting worse, reach its lowest point = ______________

level out | count out | count down | add up | ~~mount up~~ | average out (at) | bottom out

26 Success and failure

26.1 SUCCESS

Nia **built on** her experience working at a hotel to set up her own guesthouse.

build on
use your knowledge, experience, or success as a way to become more successful

Clive **muddled through** the interview without any preparation. He was shocked when he got the job.

muddle through
manage to do something despite having no plan or understanding of it

When I didn't get into college, I started my own successful business. Everything **worked out** in the end!

work out
have a positive outcome

I know these results are disappointing, but keep working and you will **win out** eventually.

win out
be successful after difficulty

Anita's hard work has **paid off**. The dress looks beautiful.

pay off
benefit after investing time or money

I never imagined James would be so great playing Hamlet, but he really **carried** it **off**.

carry off
unexpectedly succeed at something

The Scottish team **pulled off** an amazing victory, scoring two goals in the last four minutes.

pull off
be successful (despite difficulties)

Maria's dream of becoming famous finally **came off** when her song became a huge summer hit.

come off
be successful (about a plan)

Marco did not study at all for the English exam but somehow **scraped by**.

scrape by
only just succeed in doing something

Kwase **sailed through** his driving test. He didn't make any mistakes.

sail through
deal with something very easily

See also:
come off **6**, **52** give up **55** pay off **14**
run into **14** work out **20**, **33**

26.2 FAILURE

Marcello tried to fix the washing machine, but he has given up.

give up
stop trying to achieve something

Many smaller stores have lost out since the supermarket opened in town.

lose out (to)
be beaten by something else

Simon's campaign ran into difficulties when he was accused of lying.

run into
begin to experience something negative

The decorators have screwed up this job! We won't use them again.

screw up
make a mess of something (informal)

26.3 CAUSES OF SUCCESS AND FAILURE

The future success of our company rides on us winning this contract.

ride on
depend on

When accepting the award, Carla put her success down to hard work.

put down to
attribute events to a particular reason

Having supportive parents really contributed to my success.

contribute to
help to cause something

My teachers told me I'd never amount to anything, but now I'm a lawyer.

amount to
develop into (often used in the negative)

When Al saw how many people were making money by selling things online, he decided to get in on it.

get in on
become involved in a successful activity

Aa 26.4 MATCH THE DEFINITIONS TO THE CORRECT PHRASAL VERBS

	Definition	Phrasal verb
	be successful (about a plan) → come off	win out
1	only just succeed in doing something	sail through
2	unexpectedly succeed at something	come off
3	be successful after difficulty	carry off
4	deal with something very easily	run into
5	begin to experience something negative	screw up
6	stop trying to achieve something	scrape by
7	make a mess of something	give up

26.5 LISTEN TO THE AUDIO AND MARK THE PHRASAL VERBS YOU HEAR

scrape by ☑ give up ☐

1 screw up ☐ put down to ☐

2 carry off ☐ ride on ☐

3 win out ☐ win over ☐

4 come off ☐ come up ☐

5 run into ☐ run off ☐

Aa 26.6 MARK THE SENTENCES THAT ARE CORRECT

When accepting the award, Carla put her success down to hard work. ☑
When accepting the award, Carla put her success up to hard work. ☐

1 

My teachers told me I'd never add up to anything, but now I'm a lawyer. ☐
My teachers told me I'd never amount to anything, but now I'm a lawyer. ☐

2 

Anita's hard work has paid up. The dress looks beautiful. ☐
Anita's hard work has paid off. The dress looks beautiful. ☐

3 

Many smaller stores have lost out since the supermarket opened in town. ☐
Many smaller stores have closed out since the supermarket opened in town. ☐

4 

Nia looked on her experience working at a hotel to set up her own guesthouse. ☐
Nia built on her experience working at a hotel to set up her own guesthouse. ☐

5 

Having supportive parents really attributed to my success. ☐
Having supportive parents really contributed to my success. ☐

Aa 26.7 REWRITE THE SENTENCES, CORRECTING THE ERRORS

The future success of our company **drives on** us winning this contract.
The future success of our company rides on us winning this contract.

1. Clive **muddled on** the interview without any preparation. He was shocked when he got the job.

____

2. When I didn't get into college, I started my own successful business. Everything **worked up** in the end!

____

3. The Scottish team **pushed off** an amazing victory, scoring two goals in the last four minutes.

____

4. When Al saw how many people were making money by selling things online, he decided to **get out on** it.

____

5. Kwase **sailed into** his driving test. He didn't make any mistakes.

____

27 At home

27.1 PHRASAL VERBS WITH "LOCK"

Clive makes sure that he locks his tools away in his shed.

lock away
put something away and lock the door

When Ben got home, he realized that he'd forgotten his keys and was locked out.

lock out
stop someone from entering by locking the door

The janitor didn't notice Alex when he locked the doors. He accidentally locked him in.

lock in
stop someone from leaving by locking the door

27.3 APPLIANCES AND HOUSEHOLD ITEMS

Did you leave the lights on when you left the house?

leave on
leave turned on

The lights in the house went out, so Clara lit some candles.

go out
(lights) stop shining

It was a very hot day, so Les put the fan on.

put on (UK)
make a piece of equipment start working

Andy blew the candles out before going to bed.

blow out
make a candle stop burning by blowing air at it

If you're bored, turn on the television. There's a good movie on tonight.

turn on
make something start working

Make sure you turn the television off before going to bed.

turn off
make something stop working

See also:
come on **52**, **56** go off **3**, **8**, **30**, **35** go out **3**, **5**, **54**
put on **6**, **41**, **55** turn off **9** turn on **1** turn up **1**, **4**

27.2 MOVING

Pete's new neighbors moved in last weekend.

move in(to)
start living in new home

We finally sold our house. We're moving out today.

move out (of)
stop living in your old home and move somewhere else

My parents have decided to move away and live in the country.

move away
go and live in a different area

Jools has settled into his new apartment very quickly.

settle in(to)
get used to living in a new place

When Elsa heard her favorite song on the radio, she turned up the volume and began dancing.

turn up
increase the volume (or power) of a piece of equipment

Paula's neighbor asked her to turn her stereo down because it was too loud.

turn down
decrease the volume (or power) of a piece of equipment

Cassie thought her computer was broken until she realized that she hadn't plugged it in.

plug in(to)
connect an eletrical appliance to the electricity supply

The street lights come on at dusk, when the sun sets.

come on
start working (automatically)

The street lights go off at dawn, when the sun rises.

go off
stop working (automatically)

Aa 27.4 LOOK AT THE PICTURES AND COMPLETE THE SENTENCES USING THE PHRASAL VERBS IN THE PANEL

Pete's new neighbors *moved in* last weekend.

4 When Elsa heard her favorite song on the radio, she ______________ the volume.

1 If you're bored, ______________ the television. There's a good movie on tonight.

5 The street lights ______________ at dusk, when the sun sets.

2 When Ben got home, he realized that he'd forgotten his keys and was ______________ .

6 The lights in the house ______________ , so Clara lit some candles.

3 My parents have decided to ______________ and live in the country.

7 We finally sold our house. We're ______________ ______________ today.

moving out	come on	turn on	move away
locked out	~~moved in~~	turned up	went out

27.5 MATCH THE PHRASAL VERBS TO THEIR OPPOSITES

	put on	go off
1	come on	turn on
2	move out	turn off
3	lock in	move in
4	turn off	turn down
5	turn up	lock out

(Example: put on → turn off)

27.6 LISTEN TO THE AUDIO, THEN NUMBER THE PICTURES IN THE ORDER YOU HEAR THEM

A ☐

B 1

C ☐

D ☐

E ☐

F ☐

27.7 WRITE THE CORRECT PHRASAL VERB NEXT TO ITS DEFINITION

(lights) stop shining = *go out*

1. make something stop working = ______
2. stop someone from leaving by locking the door = ______
3. leave turned on = ______
4. decrease the volume of a piece of equipment = ______
5. start working (automatically) = ______

lock in | turn down | come on | ~~go out~~ | leave on | turn off

28 Chores

28.1 CLEANING

We need to tidy up before the guests arrive.

tidy up
make tidy again

Elliot's dad told him to clear away all his toys.

clear away
put things back in their proper places

Jason told me to mop up the water that I'd spilled on the floor.

mop up
clean liquid off a surface with a mop

This room is a mess! Pick up all these clothes!

pick up
take something off the floor

If the chicken smells bad, you should throw it away.

throw away
discard, put in the trash

When Ella cooks dinner, her boyfriend washes up the dishes.

wash up (UK)
clean the dishes

After painting the living room, Paul and Sally put all the furniture back.

put back
return an object to its original place

It was a sunny morning, so Ian hung his washing out to dry.

hang out
hang washing on a clothesline to dry

There was a lot of mess to clean up after the party.

clean up
make tidy again

We all pitched in to get it finished more quickly.

pitch in
join in, help others to do something

See also:
cut back **14** hang out **5** pick up **9**, **10**, **11**, **31**, **38** pull up **9**
put up **35** take out **3**, **14**, **21** throw away **31**

We cleared out the garage this weekend. There was so much junk in there!

clear out
remove all the unnecessary things from a room or building

I wipe down the table each evening after we've eaten.

wipe down
clean a surface with a cloth

On Tuesday mornings, I take the trash out.

take out
move something outside

Nousha's room looked much nicer after she'd put up some pictures.

put up
hang something on a wall

Karl swept up the trash from the party and put it into bags.

sweep up
clean the ground with a broom

28.2 GARDENING

The tree in our backyard died, so we had to chop it down.

chop down
make a tree fall to the ground

The hedge in Doug's yard was getting too big, so he cut it back.

cut back
remove some branches from a tree, bush, or hedge

I'm digging up the lavender bushes so I can move them to a different part of the garden.

dig up
remove a plant from the ground by digging around and under it

Paul spent the whole afternoon pulling up weeds. His yard was full of them.

pull up
remove a plant from ground by pulling

After finishing the gardening, Scott put his tools away.

put away
return an object to its proper place

Aa 28.3 MATCH THE DEFINITIONS TO THE CORRECT PHRASAL VERBS

take something off the floor → pick up	pull up
1 return an object to its original place	chop down
2 make a tree fall to the ground	pick up
3 join in, help others to do something	take out
4 remove a plant from the ground by pulling	wash up
5 move something outside	put back
6 remove all the unnecessary things from a room	pitch in
7 clean the dishes	clear out

Aa 28.4 CROSS OUT THE INCORRECT WORDS IN EACH SENTENCE

Elliot's dad told him to clear ~~up~~ / away / ~~out~~ all his toys.

1  Nousha's room looked much nicer after she'd put up / in / on some pictures.

2  Paul spent the whole afternoon pulling on / in / up weeds.

3  Karl swept down / over / up the trash from the party and put it into bags.

4 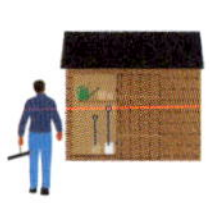 After finishing the gardening, Scott put his tools up / away / out.

5 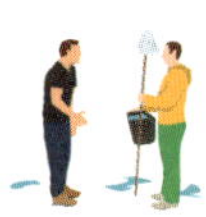 Jason told me to mop up / around / over the water that I'd spilled on the floor.

28.5 LISTEN TO THE AUDIO AND COMPLETE THE SENTENCES THAT DESCRIBE EACH PICTURE

This room is a mess! *Pick up* all these clothes!

3 I ________________ the table each evening after we've eaten.

1 The tree in our backyard died, so we had to ________________ .

4 We need to ________________ before the guests arrive.

2 I'm ________________ the lavender bushes so I can move them to a different part of the garden.

5 The hedge in Doug's yard was getting too big, so he ________________.

28.6 REWRITE THE SENTENCES, CORRECTING THE ERRORS

We all **pitched out** to get it finished quickly.
We all pitched in to get it finished quickly.

1 On Tuesday mornings, I **take** the trash **off**.

____

2 If the chicken smells bad, **throw** it **over**.

____

3 Ian **hung** his washing **in** to dry.

____

4 We **cleared over** the garage this weekend.

____

5 There was a mess to **clean on** after the party.

____

29 Cooking

29.1 COOKING

Patrick broke up the chocolate before adding it to the cake mixture.

break up

separate something into smaller pieces

Nadiya left the cherry pie on the windowsill to cool down.

cool down

become cooler

I always measure out all of my ingredients before trying a new recipe.

measure out

weigh or take a certain amount

You should mix in the eggs and milk with the other ingredients.

mix in

combine (with other ingredients)

My sister can whip up a tasty meal in minutes from just a few ingredients.

whip up

prepare (a meal) quickly

Before serving the curry I made sure to fish out any bones.

fish out

remove from a liquid

The sauce boiled over, leaving a mess on the stove top.

boil over

flow over the edge of a container (during cooking)

Dev took the leftovers from the fridge and heated them up in the microwave.

heat up

make hotter

My breakfast typically consists of bread and cheese, served with coffee.

consist of

be formed of

We managed to fill up three jars with the cookies we'd baked.

fill up

fill a container to the top

See also:
break up **3**, **15**, **21**, **38**
cool down **11.1**

29.2 PREPARING A RECIPE

RECIPE

CHICKEN CASSEROLE

INGREDIENTS

2 onions
3 carrots
5 potatoes
2 chicken thighs
1 pint vegetable stock
Chopped parsley (to garnish)

SERVES: 4

PREP TIME: 15 minutes

COOK TIME: 30 minutes

METHOD

1. Start by chopping up some onions, carrots, and potatoes, then set them aside for later.
2. Fry the meat on a medium heat for 10 minutes (you may want to cut off any extra fat from the meat).
3. Pour in the stock, add the vegetables, and boil for 20 minutes.
4. Finish off the stew by adding chopped parsley.

Note: To make a vegetarian version, leave out the meat and use mushrooms instead.

Start by chopping up some onions, carrots, and potatoes.

chop up
cut into small pieces

After you've chopped the vegetables, set them aside for later.

set aside
keep something for later

I always cut off the fat from the meat before cooking it.

cut off
remove something from a larger piece

When the meat is cooked, pour in the stock.

pour in
add a liquid

Finish off the stew by adding chopped parsley.

finish off
complete

To make a vegetarian version, leave out the meat and use mushrooms instead.

leave out
exclude, not include

Aa 29.3 FILL IN THE GAPS USING THE PHRASAL VERBS IN THE PANEL

You should ___mix in___ the eggs and milk with the other ingredients.

1. I always ________________ the fat from the meat before cooking it.
2. My breakfast typically ________________ bread and cheese, served with coffee.
3. Nadiya left the cherry pie on the windowsill to ________________.
4. Before serving the curry I made sure to ________________ any bones.
5. My sister can ________________ a tasty meal in minutes from just a few ingredients.

cool down	~~mix in~~	cut off	whip up	fish out	consists of

29.4 LISTEN TO THE AUDIO AND MARK THE PHRASAL VERBS YOU HEAR

measure out ☑
measure over ☐

1. chop off ☐
   chop up ☐

2. set apart ☐
   set aside ☐

3. cut off ☐
   cut away ☐

4. mix up ☐
   mix in ☐

5. pour in ☐
   pour over ☐

6. finish off ☐
   finish up ☐

7. fish out ☐
   fish for ☐

8. cool off ☐
   cool down ☐

9. leave out ☐
   leave in ☐

29.5 MATCH THE PICTURES TO THE CORRECT SENTENCES

1 

2 

3 

4 

5 

- The sauce boiled over, leaving a mess on the stove top.
- Dev took the leftovers from the fridge and heated them up in the microwave.
- I always measure out all of my ingredients before trying a new recipe.
- Patrick broke up the chocolate before adding it to the cake mixture.
- We managed to fill up three jars with the cookies we'd baked.
- My sister can whip up a tasty meal in minutes from just a few ingredients.

29.6 REWRITE THE SENTENCES, CORRECTING THE ERRORS

Start by **chopping ups** onions and carrots.
Start by chopping up onions and carrots.

1 After chopping the vegetables, **set** them **beside**.

____

2 **Cut on** the fat from the meat before cooking it.

____

3 When the meat is cooked, **pour up** the stock.

____

4 **Mix over** the eggs with the other ingredients.

____

5 **Finish in** the stew by adding chopped parsley.

____

6 Before serving, make sure to **fish on** any bones.

____

7 For a vegetarian version, **leave down** the meat.

____

30 Food and drink

30.1 FOOD

Rosa served up a wonderful seafood dish.

serve up
present food to other people

Martin's grandmother told him he could only have dessert if he ate up all his vegetables.

eat up
eat all of something

Selma and Roy prefer to eat in. It's much cheaper than going to a restaurant.

eat in
eat a meal at home

That fish really didn't agree with me. I have a terrible stomachache.

not agree with
make someone feel ill

I think this milk has gone off. It smells terrible.

go off (UK)
become bad to eat or drink

Apple pie and ice cream go together perfectly.

go together
taste or look good together

Our restaurant can cater for about 100 customers at a time.

cater for
provide for

30.2 DRINK

After the wedding, we all drank to the bride and groom.

drink to
toast someone or something

The café was about to close, so we drank up and got ready to leave.

drink up
drink all of something

See also:
break off **49** go off **8**, **27**, **35**
run out (of) **15** take away **25**, **55**

I was going to make a lasagna, but we've **run out of** pasta.

Why don't we **eat out** for a change? We could go to that new Italian restaurant instead.

run out (of)
use all of something, not have any more of something

eat out
eat in a café or restaurant, eat away from home

Daniel broke off a piece of bread and dipped it in the olive oil.

break off
separate a smaller piece of something from a larger piece

Lisa shared out the chocolates, giving the children two each.

share out
give each person the same amount of something

Greg was so hungry that he polished off the entire cake.

polish off
eat or drink all of something

After a long day at the beach, my kids wolfed down their dinner.

wolf down
eat all of something very quickly

Paul and Sarah ordered two hamburgers and sodas to take away.

take away (UK)
take food out of a restaurant to eat

This cake is delicious, but it could do without all the cream on top.

do without
be better without

I washed down my pizza with a cold drink.

wash down
drink something after eating (informal)

Your mug's almost empty, Peter. Would you like me to top it up?

top up
fill a cup or glass that is partly empty

30.3 MATCH THE BEGINNINGS OF THE SENTENCES TO THE CORRECT ENDINGS

Greg was so hungry that → he polished off the entire cake.

1. I washed down my pizza
2. Our restaurant can cater for
3. After the wedding,
4. Lisa shared out the chocolates,
5. I was going to make a lasagna,

- we all drank to the bride and groom.
- giving the children two each.
- he polished off the entire cake.
- but we've run out of pasta.
- about 100 customers at a time.
- with a cold drink.

30.4 CROSS OUT THE INCORRECT WORDS IN EACH SENTENCE

After the wedding, we all drank ~~on~~ / to / ~~over~~ the bride and groom.

1.  Paul and Sarah ordered two hamburgers and sodas to take away / off / with.

2.  The café was about to close, so we drank down / in / up and got ready to leave.

3.  I washed up / down / in my pizza with a cold drink.

4.  After a long day at the beach, my kids wolfed out / down / on their dinner.

5.  Daniel broke over / off / down a piece of bread and dipped it in the olive oil.

30.5 LISTEN TO THE AUDIO AND MARK THE PHRASAL VERBS YOU HEAR

serve up ☑
serve over ☐

1. run out of ☐
   run down ☐

2. go on ☐
   go off ☐

3. eat up ☐
   eat down ☐

4. wash down ☐
   wash up ☐

5. go together ☐
   go with ☐

30.6 WRITE THE CORRECT PHRASAL VERB NEXT TO ITS DEFINITION, FILLING IN THE MISSING LETTERS

eat or drink all of something = p o l i s h o f f

1. eat away from home = e _ _ o _ _
2. fill a cup or glass that is partly empty = t _ _ u _
3. toast someone or something = d _ _ _ _ t _
4. eat a meal at home = e _ _ i _
5. taste or look good together = g _ t _ _ _ _ _ _ _

31 Free time

31.1 HOBBIES

Anastasia absolutely lives for skiing. She goes to the mountains whenever she can.

live for
have a passion for, consider something the most important thing in your life

I recently got back into cycling. I hadn't done it since I was a teenager.

get back into
start doing something again after not doing it for some time

It takes a while to get into horseback riding.

get into
become interested in, begin to enjoy an activity

It's hard at first, but if you keep at it you'll start to love it.

keep at
keep practicing a skill or activity

Adi's painting skills are really coming along. He might become an artist one day.

come along
improve at a skill or activity

After she retired, Kim took up yoga. She does it for half an hour each morning.

take up
start learning a new skill or activity

31.2 RELAXING

Nathan told his daughters to stop lazing about, and help to tidy the house.

laze about
relax, do no work

After the exam, the students went to the local park to wind down.

wind down
become calm (after a period of work or excitement)

On my days off work, I like to sit around the garden doing nothing.

sit around
spend time sitting, doing little

I spend most Sundays lying around the house.

lie around
relax on the couch or in bed

See also: come along **5**, **52** get into **23** get out of **17** pick up **9**, **10**, **11**, **28**, **38** take up **15**, **55** throw away **28** wind down **23**

Learning the piano isn't easy, but if you stick at it, you could become a great pianist.

stick at (UK)
keep practicing a skill or activity despite difficulties

Ken's currently working toward getting a black belt in judo.

work toward
invest time in something with the aim of achieving something

While working in Seoul I tried to pick up some Korean by talking to local people.

pick up
learn a new skill informally

Fabio could have been a great guitarist, but he threw it all away by never practicing.

throw away
waste a talent or opportunity

If you want to be a great tennis player, it helps if you start out at a young age.

start out
begin doing a hobby or career

I found running very hard when I started, but I get a lot of satisfaction out of it now.

get out of
enjoy

Luiza spent the evening curled up on the couch reading a book.

curl up
lie or sit with your arms and legs pulled up towards you

Aden needs to loosen up. Tell him to come and dance with us!

loosen up
relax, stop being so formal

After a stressful day, I take a bath to help me chill out.

chill out
relax, stop feeling angry or stressed

On Friday evenings, Josh likes to kick back and watch some television.

kick back
stop work and relax (informal)

Aa 31.3 CROSS OUT THE INCORRECT WORDS IN EACH SENTENCE

It takes a while to get into / ~~behind~~ / ~~above~~ horseback riding.

1. Ken's currently working around / toward / for getting a black belt in judo.
2. Nathan told his daughters to stop lazing beside / about / along, and help to tidy the house.
3. After the exam, the students went to the local park to wind low / below / down.
4. I recently got back into / onto / for cycling. I hadn't done it since I was a teenager.
5. On Friday evenings, Josh likes to kick ahead / back / around and watch some television.
6. Anastasia absolutely lives by / on / for skiing. She goes to the mountains whenever she can.

Aa 31.4 MATCH THE PICTURES TO THE CORRECT SENTENCES

1 

2 

3 

4 

I found running very hard when I started, but I get a lot of satisfaction out of it now.

While working in Seoul I tried to pick up some Korean by talking to local people.

Fabio could have been a great guitarist, but he threw it all away by never practicing.

Learning the piano isn't easy, but if you stick at it, you could become a great pianist.

Adi's painting skills are really coming along. He might become an artist one day.

31.5 LISTEN TO THE AUDIO AND MATCH THE IMAGES TO THE CORRECT PHRASAL VERBS

1

2

3

4

sit around

take up

live for

start out

curl up

31.6 REWRITE THE SENTENCES, PUTTING THE WORDS IN THE CORRECT ORDER

keep | you | it. | at | love | you'll | If | to | start | it,

If you keep at it, you'll start to love it.

the | around | I | most | spend | Sundays | lying | house.

1 ______________________________

loosen | us. | to | and | Aden | dance | with | needs | up

2 ______________________________

On | off, | I | around | to | sit | the | my | days | like | garden.

3 ______________________________

curled | Louiza | evening | up | the | spent | couch. | on | the

4 ______________________________

I | chill | After | stressful | take | bath | a | to | a | out. | day,

5 ______________________________

32 Health

32.1 HEALTH

My son always bounces back quickly whenever he gets ill.

bounce back
to recover quickly or without difficulty

The wound seems to be healing up well. It will be better soon.

heal up (UK)
(about a wound) become completely healthy

Elaine's rash began to clear up after she started using the cream.

clear up
go away or get better

My brother's a nurse. He cares for sick people at the local hospital.

care for
take care of

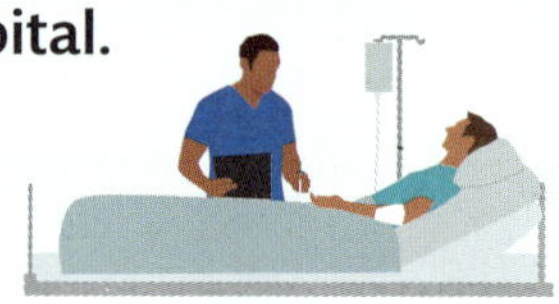

There's a bad cold going around my office at the moment. Everyone is ill.

go around
spread from person to person

Mona has an awful headache. She doesn't feel up to working today.

feel up to
feel in a good enough condition

Paola's hay fever usually flares up in the spring.

flare up
suddenly appear or reappear

It's taken me weeks to get over this cold, but I finally feel better.

get over
recover, feel well again

Danny's thumb swelled up after he was stung by a wasp.

swell up
(about a swelling) become bigger

After a few hours, the swelling had started to go down.

go down
(about a swelling) become smaller

See also:
care for **3** clear up **11**, **50** get over **45, 53**
go around **54** go down **12**, **54** pass on **38**

I think I'm coming down with the flu. I have a headache and my nose is running.

come down with
become ill with

When Rachel came around after the operation, her husband was sitting at her bedside.

come around
become conscious again

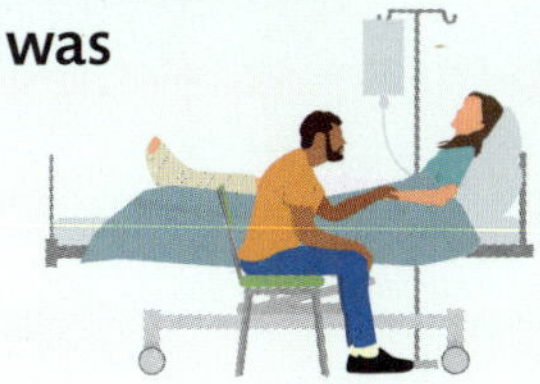

I was very sad to hear that your grandmother has passed away.

pass away
die

My son passed on the virus to his sisters.

pass on
give (an illness) to someone else

One of the musicians passed out during the performance this evening.

pass out
faint, become unconscious

It was a very risky operation, but Josh pulled through.

pull through
survive a serious illness or operation

Tina's leg muscles seized up after she had completed the marathon.

seize up
become stiff, difficult to move

I've been ill for weeks, but I've finally managed to shake it off.

shake off
fully recover from

Ella's been throwing up all day. She must be suffering from food poisoning.

throw up
vomit

As the painkiller wore off, Shahid's tooth began to ache again.

wear off
gradually lose its effectiveness

32.2 MATCH THE DEFINITIONS TO THE CORRECT PHRASAL VERBS

to recover quickly or without difficulty → bounce back	heal up
1 become completely healthy	throw up
2 vomit	bounce back
3 suddenly appear or reappear	go around
4 become conscious again	seize up
5 become stiff, difficult to move	come around
6 spread from person to person	flare up

32.3 CROSS OUT THE INCORRECT WORDS IN EACH SENTENCE

It was a very risky operation, but Josh pulled ~~under~~ / ~~over~~ / through.

1  Elaine's rash began to clear out / in / up after she started using the cream.

2  I think I'm coming down with / for / to the flu.

3  Ella's been throwing over / up / down all day.

4  My son passed over / through / on the virus to his sisters.

5  It's taken me weeks to get over / around / through this cold, but I finally feel better.

32.4 LISTEN TO THE AUDIO AND COMPLETE THE SENTENCES THAT DESCRIBE EACH PICTURE

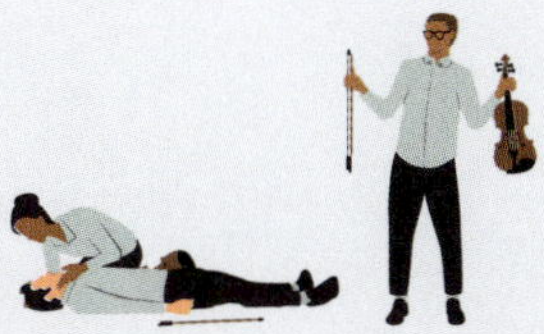

One of the musicians *passed out* during the performance this evening.

3 Danny's thumb ______________ after he was stung by a wasp.

1 Paola's hay fever usually ______________ in the spring.

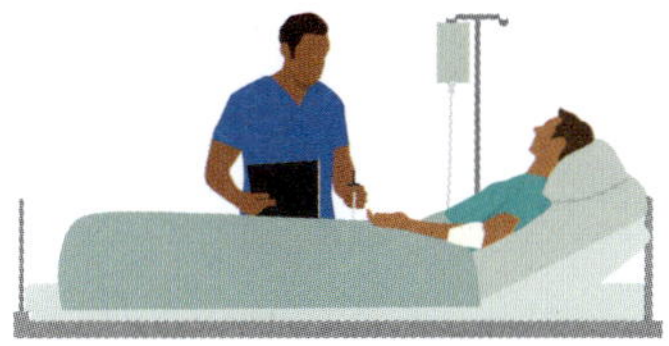

4 My brother's a nurse. He ______________ sick people at the local hospital.

2 After a few hours, the swelling had started to ______________ .

5 I was very sad to hear that your grandmother has ______________ .

32.5 WRITE THE CORRECT PHRASAL VERB NEXT TO ITS DEFINITION

become stiff, difficult to move = *seize up*

1 take care of = ______________

2 feel in a good enough condition = ______________

3 spread from person to person = ______________

4 gradually lose its effectiveness = ______________

5 survive a serious illness or operation = ______________

33 Sports and exercise

33.1 SPORTS

Clara was sent off the pitch after pushing over another player.

send off
tell someone to leave a game because they have broken the rules

Angela knocked Kirsten out in the first round of the competition.

knock out (of)
defeat a team or player, removing them from a competition

The crowd cheered Tony on as he approached the finish line.

cheer on
encourage someone by cheering

Pete wanted to start playing baseball, so he signed up for his school team.

sign up (for)
join a team or activity

My sister is a judo champion. She ranks among the best in the country.

rank among
be included among

Five runners have gotten through to the final. Whoever wins this race gets the trophy.

get through (to)
reach (a stage in a competition)

33.2 EXERCISE

After a big meal, Chris goes for a brisk walk to burn off the extra calories.

burn off
use up energy (by doing exercise)

For this yoga position, you have to stretch your arms out as far as you can.

stretch out
extend

Playing tennis all afternoon with Gus has worn Charlie out.

wear out
make very tired

Jamal was completely wiped out after cycling up the mountain.

wipe out
make extremely tired

See also:
aim at **34** get through (to) **38** keep from **51** keep up (with) **20** send off **38**
turn around **19** warm up **11** wear out **49** work out **20**, **26**

Frank watched Phillip play tennis. He was sizing up his opponent before the next day's match.

size up
look (at a person or situation) and decide how to act

It looked like the Eagles were going to lose the match, but they turned it around at the last minute.

turn around
make a bad situation better

I picked up my bow and aimed another arrow at the target.

aim at
direct something at something else

Sami invited me to join in a game of cricket.

join in
get involved in something that others are already doing

My knee injury kept me from completing the marathon this year.

keep from
prevent someone from doing something

I struggle to keep up with my brother. He's much fitter than I am.

keep up (with)
move at the same speed

After a long day in the office, playing squash helps me to work off all my stress.

work off
get rid of (energy or an emotion)

After finishing the race, Sandra warmed down by stretching her legs.

warm down
stretch and relax your body after exercise

Before playing a game of soccer, I always warm up by jogging slowly.

warm up
prepare your body for exercise

Leo works out at his local gym every morning.

work out
exercise

Aa 33.3 FILL IN THE GAPS USING THE WORDS IN THE PANEL TO CREATE PHRASAL VERBS

After a big meal, Chris goes for a brisk walk to [burn *off*] the extra calories.

1. After finishing the race, Sandra [warmed] by stretching her legs.
2. Jamal was completely [wiped] after cycling up the mountain.
3. Clara was [sent] the pitch after pushing over another player.
4. Five runners have [gotten] to the final. Whoever wins this race will win the trophy.
5. My sister is a judo champion. She [ranks] the best in the country.
6. I struggle to [keep] with my brother. He's much fitter than I am.

out	among	~~off~~	through	up	down	off

Aa 33.4 MARK THE SENTENCES THAT ARE CORRECT

Playing tennis all afternoon with Gus has worn Charlie out. ☑
Playing tennis all afternoon with Gus has worn Charlie off. ☐

1. 

   Before playing a game of soccer, I always warm down by jogging slowly. ☐
   Before playing a game of soccer, I always warm up by jogging slowly. ☐

2. 

   For this yoga position, you have to stretch your arms out as far as you can. ☐
   For this yoga position, you have to stretch your arms in as far as you can. ☐

3. 

   Pete wanted to start playing baseball, so he signed on for his school team. ☐
   Pete wanted to start playing baseball, so he signed up for his school team. ☐

4. 

   Angela knocked Kirsten out in the first round of the competition. ☐
   Angela knocked Kirsten down in the first round of the competition. ☐

5. 

   My knee injury kept me through completing the marathon this year. ☐
   My knee injury kept me from completing the marathon this year. ☐

33.5 LISTEN TO THE AUDIO AND WRITE THE SENTENCES BELOW THE IMAGES

Sami invited me to join in a game of cricket.

1 ______________________________

2 ______________________________

3 ______________________________

4 ______________________________

5 ______________________________

33.6 WRITE THE CORRECT PHRASAL VERB NEXT TO ITS DEFINITION

direct something at something else	=	aim at
1 move at the same speed	=	______
2 prepare your body for exercise	=	______
3 look (at a person or situation) and decide how to act	=	______
4 make a bad situation better	=	______
5 use up energy (by doing exercise)	=	______
6 encourage someone by cheering	=	______
7 get rid of (energy or an emotion)	=	______

34 The arts

See also:
aim at 33

34.1 CREATIVITY

Sami and Shahid made the cardboard box into a robot.

make into
change something into something else

The architects have mocked up a model of the new museum.

mock up
make a model of something

Greg and Chloe colored in pictures of dinosaurs after their trip to the museum.

color in
use colored pencils or pens to add colors to a drawing

34.2 MEDIA

The new music channel is aimed at people who like jazz.

aim at
be intended for or targeted at

This new TV show feeds on people's curiosity about aliens.

feed on
take advantage of

I tune into my favorite radio show every Sunday morning.

tune into
watch or listen to a program or station on the television or radio

34.3 MUSIC

At the start of the horror movie, scary music started to fade in.

fade in
gradually become louder

The noise from the parade faded away as it moved away from us.

fade away
gradually become quieter

As the music died away, the presenter stepped onto the stage.

die away
become quieter before ending

My new headphones help me concentrate by filtering out background noise.

filter out
remove or block something

Aa 34.4 FILL IN THE GAPS USING THE PHRASAL VERBS IN THE PANEL

As the music *died away*, the presenter stepped onto the stage.

1. The new music channel is ________ people who like jazz.
2. At the start of the horror movie, scary music started to ________ .
3. My new headphones help me concentrate by ________ background noise.
4. This new TV show ________ people's curiosity about aliens.
5. The noise from the parade ________ as it moved away from us.
6. I ________ my favorite radio show every Sunday morning.

feeds on | fade in | ~~died away~~ | tune into | filtering out | aimed at | faded away

34.5 LISTEN TO THE AUDIO AND WRITE THE SENTENCES BELOW THE IMAGES

Sami and Shahid made the cardboard box into a robot.

1. ________

2. ________

3. ________

4. ________

5. ________

35 Travel

See also: arrive at **47** bring back **16** check out **10**, **50** end up **17** get around **50**, **53** get away **13** get back (from) **1** go back **16**, **54** go off **3**, **8**, **27**, **30** put up **28** set off **46**, **53** set out **23**, **53**

35.1 TRAVEL

When Krishna arrived at the villa, the party had already begun.

arrive at
reach a destination

During his vacation in Rome, Anton hired a moped to get around the city.

get around
travel from place to place

When they arrived at the hotel, Julia and John went to reception to check in.

check in(to)
register your arrival at a hotel or airport

Julia and John checked out of the hotel and went to the airport.

check out (of)
leave a hotel after paying the bill

On your way to London you'll pass by Cambridge, a beautiful university city.

pass by
pass another place (while on the way somewhere else)

Dan and I went to Paris for our honeymoon. We went back last month for our 25th wedding anniversary.

go back
visit again

By the time we got back from our cycle ride, it was already getting dark.

get back from
return from

We were supposed to hike to the mountain, but we ended up by the lake.

end up
arrive somewhere unintentionally

Marimar and I went off to Miami recently.

go off (to)
go on a trip or vacation

It was great to get away for a few days!

get away
go somewhere for a break or to relax

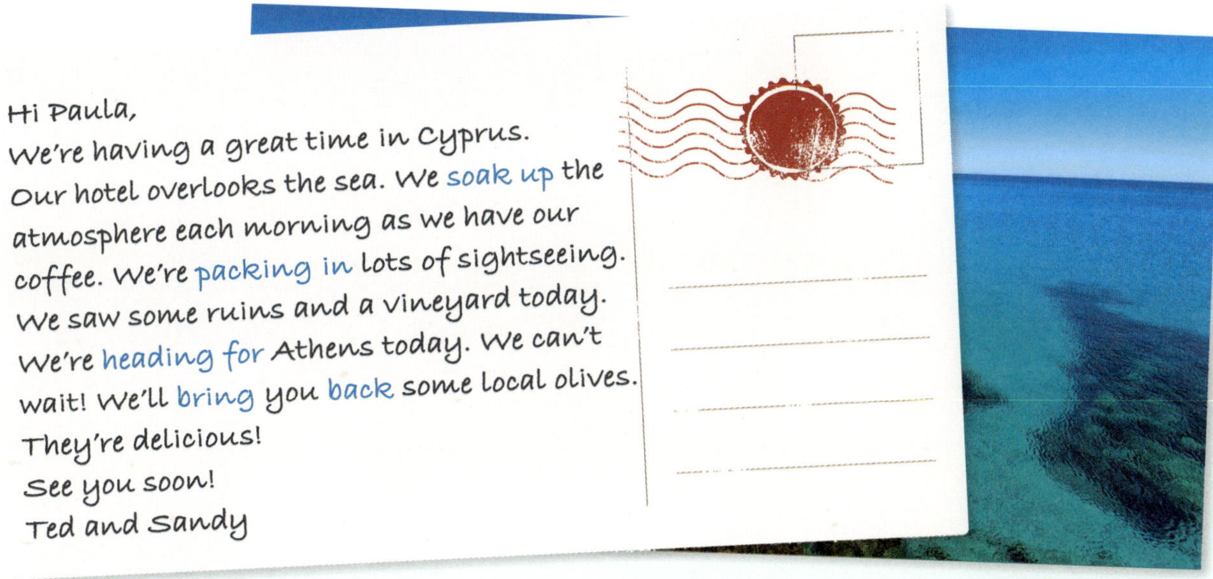

Our hotel overlooks the sea. We soak up the atmosphere each morning as we have our coffee.

soak up
look and listen, enjoy

We're packing in lots of sightseeing during our vacation. We saw some ruins and a vineyard today.

pack in
include (a lot of something)

We've been in Cyprus for a few days, but we're heading for Athens today.

head for
move towards a certain destination

We brought you back some local olives. They're delicious!

bring back
return with

Whenever we set out on a hike, we always take waterproofs, a compass, and a map.

set out (on)
start a journey

We set off for Chicago at dawn when there would be less traffic on the roads.

set off (for)
start a journey

On our way to Barcelona, we stopped over in a lovely hotel for the night.

stop over
stay somewhere on the way to somewhere else

We managed to put the tent up even though it was raining heavily.

put up
put together, erect

35.2 LISTEN TO THE AUDIO AND MARK THE PHRASAL VERBS YOU HEAR

get away ☑ get up ☐

1 get under ☐ get around ☐

2 check on ☐ check in ☐

3 get back from ☐ get back to ☐

4 put out ☐ put up ☐

5 soak in ☐ soak up ☐

35.3 REWRITE THE SENTENCES, PUTTING THE WORDS IN THE CORRECT ORDER

to | get | Anton | moped | around | the | hired | city. | a

Anton hired a moped to get around the city.

brought | olives. | We | you | local | back | some

1 ______________________________

hotel. | They | out | the | checked | of

2 ______________________________

Miami | I | and | off | Marimar | recently. | went | to

3 ______________________________

great | away | days! | get | few | a | for | It | to | was

4 ______________________________

35.4 MATCH THE BEGINNINGS OF THE SENTENCES TO THE CORRECT ENDINGS

During his vacation in Rome, → Anton hired a moped to get around the city.

1. On our way to Barcelona,
2. Whenever we set out on a hike,
3. We set off for Chicago at dawn
4. When she arrived at the hotel,
5. We managed to put the tent up

- we stopped over in a hotel for the night.
- Julia went to the reception to check in.
- Anton hired a moped to get around the city.
- even though it was raining heavily.
- we always take a compass and a map.
- when there would be less traffic.

35.5 FILL IN THE GAPS USING THE PHRASAL VERBS IN THE PANEL

By the time we *got back from* our cycle ride, it was dark.

1. When Krishna __________ the villa, the party had begun.

2. We're __________ lots of sightseeing during our vacation.

3. It was great to __________ for a few days.

4. We've been in Cyprus all week, but we're __________ Athens today.

5. On your way to London, you'll __________ Cambridge.

arrived at
pass by
heading for
~~got back from~~
get away
packing in

36 Talking

36.1 TALKING

Ben's not keen on buying a new car. I'm trying to talk him round.

talk round (UK)
manage to persuade someone

Marco is always talking at people. He never gives them a chance to speak.

talk at
talk to someone without letting them speak

Shona wanted to dye her hair green, but her sister talked her out of it.

talk out of
persuade someone not to do something

Uncle Toby still talks down to me like I'm a child, even though I'm 25.

talk down to
talk in a patronizing way to

We were chatting about movies when Tina launched into a speech about her favorite actors.

launch into
suddenly begin speaking with enthusiasm about something

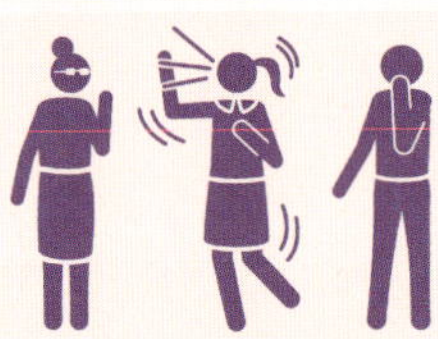

Kirsty talked the workers through the new software system.

talk through
explain how something works

My kids talked me into getting a puppy. They've promised to take care of it.

talk into
persuade someone to do something

Every time Rita tries to say something, Greg talks over her.

talk over
talk loudly while someone else is talking

While Julia was explaining her idea, Rupert cut in to tell her she was wrong.

cut in
interrupt

Simone spent the whole of lunch mouthing off about how much she hates her new boss.

mouth off
talk negatively about something or someone (informal)

See also:
blurt out **51** come up **16, 50, 52**
talk over **22**

Shut up and listen to me for once!

I think you should tone down your language.

shut up
stop talking (rude)

tone down
make your language less strong

I couldn't hear Louise at all. The man next to us was completely drowning her out.

drown out
talk louder than someone else

Lauren comes out with the funniest things. Today she told me she wants to live on the Moon.

come out with
say something surprising

Diana is always rambling on about how things were better when she was a child.

ramble on
talk for a long time about something (in an annoying or incoherent way)

The lecturer droned on for what felt like hours. We were half asleep by the end.

drone on
talk for a long time in a very boring way

Craig was trying to tell a joke, but tailed off as he realized that no one was listening.

tail off
stop talking gradually

After the concert, I struck up a conversation with one of the guitarists.

strike up
start a conversation

When soccer came up in conversation, Bill and I realized we support the same team.

come up (in)
be mentioned in conversation, usually unexpectedly

Andy blurted out the name of the winner. It was supposed to be a secret.

blurt out
say something without thinking about it first

36.2 MATCH THE BEGINNINGS OF THE SENTENCES TO THE CORRECT ENDINGS

Every time Rita tries to say something, → Greg talks over her.

1. Kirsty talked the workers
2. Shona wanted to dye her hair purple,
3. Diana is always rambling on about
4. Uncle Toby still talks down to me
5. Shut up
6. My kids talked me into

- through the new software system.
- getting a puppy.
- Greg talks over her.
- and listen to me for once!
- how things were better when she was a child.
- like I'm a child, even though I'm 25.
- but her sister talked her out of it.

36.3 MATCH THE VERBS TO THE CORRECT PARTICLES TO MAKE PHRASAL VERBS

strike → up

1. drown
2. mouth
3. ramble
4. tone
5. talk
6. launch

- down
- into
- up
- out
- on
- through
- off

36.4 LISTEN TO THE AUDIO, THEN NUMBER THE PICTURES IN THE ORDER YOU HEAR THEM

A ☐

B [1]

C ☐

D ☐

E ☐

F ☐

Aa 36.5 FILL IN THE GAPS USING THE PHRASAL VERBS IN THE PANEL

Uncle Toby still *talks down to* me like I'm a child, even though I'm 25. 

1. I think you should ______ your language. 
2. Andy ______ the name of the winner by mistake. 
3. The lecturer ______ for what felt like hours. 
4. Marco is always ______ people and not letting them speak. 
5. After the concert, I ______ a conversation with the guitarist. 

droned on
struck up
~~talks down to~~
talking at
tone down
blurted out

Aa 36.6 REWRITE THE SENTENCES, CORRECTING THE ERRORS

Lauren **goes out with** the funniest things. Today she told me she wants to live on the Moon.
Lauren comes out with the funniest things. Today she told me she wants to live on the Moon.

1. Ben's not keen on buying a new car. I'm trying to **talk** him **straight**.

______

2. When soccer **came down in** conversation, Bill and I realized we support the same team.

______

3. Craig was trying to tell a joke, but **tailed up** as he realized that no one was listening.

______

4. While Julia was explaining her idea, Rupert **chopped in** to tell her she was wrong.

______

5. Simone spent the whole of lunch **teething off** about how much she hates her new boss.

______

37 Reading and writing

37.1 WRITING

Before you can use the gym, you need to fill in this form.

fill in
complete a form

Miguel scribbled down a note to his housemate to say that he was going out for the evening.

scribble down
write something quickly or roughly

Ted always writes out his essays instead of typing them.

write out
write something in full by hand

Celia read through her notes from today's lecture and typed them up.

type up
type something from written notes

The journalist jotted down the details as Dan described his role in the new movie.

jot down
make written notes quickly

37.2 READING

I've only dipped into Nia's new novel, but it's fantastic so far.

dip into
read short parts of a book or text

What does UFO mean?

It stands for Unidentified Flying Object.

stand for
represent, be an abbreviation for

We pored over the old document looking for clues.

pore over
read with great attention

***Adventures in the Wilderness* should make for interesting reading!**

make for
result in

See also:
cut out **9** fill in **40** make for **52**

Your essay's too long, Marcel. You need to cut it down a bit.

Okay. I'll try to cut out 500 words.

cut down
reduce in size

cut out
remove material from a text

When I write a restaurant review I usually write down a few thoughts while I'm eating.

write down
record information by writing it

I write up my review at home later that evening.

write up
write or type something in full from notes

When completing the form, Damian wrote in his age.

write in
enter information by writing it

Paco read the book and noted down the most important points.

note down
make written notes

Alexandra flicked through a magazine while she waited to get her hair cut.

flick through
look through a book or magazine quickly or casually

Max read through the full report before giving his opinion.

read through
read something from start to finish

As the judge read out the names of the winners, Pablo waited hopefully.

read out
read aloud (for others to hear)

Fatima read up on ancient Greece before her history exam.

read up on
research or revise a topic

37.3 MATCH THE PHRASAL VERBS TO THE CORRECT DEFINITIONS

	Phrasal verb	Definition
	read out → read aloud (for others to hear)	write something quickly or roughly
1	note down	read with great attention
2	cut down	read aloud (for others to hear)
3	write up	complete a form
4	scribble down	write or type something in full from notes
5	stand for	reduce in size
6	pore over	represent, be an abbreviation for
7	fill in	make written notes

37.4 MARK THE SENTENCES THAT ARE CORRECT

I've only dipped into Nia's new novel, but it's fantastic so far. ☑

I've only dipped over Nia's new novel, but it's fantastic so far. ☐

1 

Before you can use the gym, you need to fill in this form. ☐

Before you can use the gym, you need to fill on this form. ☐

2 

As the judge read in the names of the winners, Pablo waited hopefully. ☐

As the judge read out the names of the winners, Pablo waited hopefully. ☐

3 

When completing the form, Damian wrote on his age. ☐

When completing the form, Damian wrote in his age. ☐

4 

Alexandra flicked through a magazine while she waited to get her hair cut. ☐

Alexandra flicked above a magazine while she waited to get her hair cut. ☐

Aa 37.5 LOOK AT THE PICTURES AND COMPLETE THE SENTENCES USING THE PHRASAL VERBS IN THE PANEL

Miguel *scribbled down* a note to his housemate to say that he was going out.

3 "UFO" ________________ Unidentified Flying Object.

1 Max ________________ the full report before giving his opinion.

4 The journalist ________________ the details as Dan described his role in the new movie.

2 Ted always ________________ his essays instead of typing them.

5 Fatima ________________ on ancient Greece before her history exam.

stands for	~~scribbled down~~	read up	writes out	jotted down	read through

Aa 37.6 FILL IN THE GAPS USING THE WORDS IN THE PANEL TO CREATE PHRASAL VERBS

When I write a restaurant review, I usually write *down* a few thoughts while I'm eating.

1 I'll try to cut ________ 500 words from my essay if it is too long.

2 *Adventures in the Wilderness* should make ________ interesting reading!

3 Paco read the book and noted ________ the most important points.

4 We pored ________ the old document looking for clues.

for	out	~~down~~	over	down

38 Keeping in touch

See also: break up **3**, **15**, **21**, **29** get through (to) **33** hang up **6** pass on **32** pick up **9**, **10**, **11**, **28**, **31** put through **55** send off **33**

38.1 ON THE PHONE

I had to call Megan six times before she finally picked up the phone.

pick up
answer a phone call

Hi Laura, sorry I'm cooking at the moment. Can I call you back in 10 minutes?

call back
return a call, phone someone who tried to speak to you earlier

Anna works from home on Tuesdays, so she will dial into the meeting.

dial in(to)
join a conference call

After chatting for over an hour, Simon and I said goodbye and hung up.

hang up
end a phone call (often suddenly)

Could you please speak up? I can't hear you very well!

speak up
talk more loudly

I've called Olly a few times this evening, but I can't get through.

get through (to)
make contact with someone by phone

Sorry, I can't hear you very well, I'm afraid. You keep breaking up.

break up
become difficult to hear (because of a bad signal or connection)

I phoned around to ask if any of my friends wanted to go to the beach with me.

phone around
phone several people

Could I speak to Mr. Yamamoto, please?

Certainly. I'll put you through now, madam.

put through (to)
connect someone to the person they want to speak to

38.2 LEAVING A MESSAGE

Hi Ulrika,
Rob called and asked me to pass on a message. He wants to follow up on your chat about the new logo last week. Can you get back to him as soon as you can?
Dave

Dave passed on a message telling me that Rob had called.

pass on
give someone a message that someone else has given to you

Rob wants to follow up on the conversation we had about the new logo.

follow up on
find out more information, do something in response to something

He asked me to get back to him as soon as possible.

get back (to)
reply to a phone call or email, contact someone (with a response to a question)

38.3 SENDING AND REPLYING

I love receiving letters from my dad. I always write back immediately.

write back
reply by letter or email

Claudia sent wedding invitations out to all her friends and family.

send out (to)
send to a group of people

I sent Paul a text asking him where he was. He texted back saying he was on the train.

text back
reply by text message

Chris emailed me a week ago, but I only just remembered to email him back.

email back
reply by email

Our company is trying to reach out to new customers by offering discounts.

reach out (to)
contact

Murat completed all the forms and sent them off to the passport office.

send off (to)
send something by post or email

Aa 38.4 CROSS OUT THE INCORRECT WORDS IN EACH SENTENCE

I had to call Megan six times before she finally picked ~~out~~ / ~~over~~ / up the phone.

1. Rob wants to chase / follow / catch up on the conversation we had about the new logo.
2. Claudia sent wedding invitations up / off / out to all her friends and family.
3. Dave passed up / off / on a message telling me that Rob had called.
4. Sorry, I can't hear you very well, I'm afraid. You keep crumbling / breaking / tearing up.
5. I've called Olly a few times this evening, but I can't get among / into / through.
6. Could you please speak down / on / up ? I can't hear you very well!

Aa 38.5 MATCH THE PICTURES TO THE CORRECT SENTENCES

1. 
2. 
3. 
4. 

Murat completed all the forms and sent them off to the passport office.

I sent Paul a text asking him where he was. He texted back saying he was on the train.

Claudia sent wedding invitations out to all her friends and family.

Chris emailed me a week ago, but I only just remembered to email him back.

I love receiving letters from my dad. I always write back immediately.

38.6 LISTEN TO THE AUDIO AND MATCH THE IMAGES TO THE CORRECT PHRASAL VERBS

1 

2 

3 

4 

pick up

hang up

speak up

put through

call back

38.7 FILL IN THE GAPS, PUTTING THE WORDS IN THE CORRECT ORDER

back | get | to

He asked me to *get* *back* *to* him as soon as possible.

the | into | dial

1 Anna works from home on Tuesdays, so she will ______ ______ ______ meeting.

through | you | put

2 I'll ______ ______ ______ to Mr. Yamamoto now, madam.

reach | to | out

3 Our company is trying to ______ ______ ______ new customers by offering discounts.

up | hung | and

4 After chatting for over an hour, Simon and I said goodbye ______ ______ ______ .

back | you | call

5 Hi Laura, sorry I'm cooking at the moment, can I ______ ______ ______ in 10 minutes?

39 Thoughts and ideas

See also: come across **1**, **52**
think through **50**
throw out **17**

39.1 IDEAS

They bombarded us with too much information during the training course.

bombard with
ask too many questions, give too much information

Gill and the design team are bouncing ideas off each other before the show next week.

bounce off
exchange creative ideas to see how other people respond to them

The president's speech touched on the economy, healthcare, and education.

touch on
briefly mention something in a talk or text

I wrote a proposal for more environmentally friendly policies and put it to the directors.

put to
make a suggestion so that others can choose to accept it or not

When my husband suggested buying a new kitchen, I ran with it.

run with
do what someone suggests

When I told my friends I was starting my own business, they all got behind the idea.

get behind
offer support to someone

The creative manager asked her team to throw out as many ideas as they could.

throw out
suggest lots of spontaneous ideas

We have ruled out three of the candidates. It's a choice between Danny and Carmen.

rule out
remove someone or something as an option when making a choice

Ted has come up with some good ideas for a new logo.

come up with
think of an idea, suggestion, or plan

He decided to put forward the version with the star.

put forward
offer an opinion, idea, or suggestion

39.2 REALIZING THINGS

The artist's feelings of anger come across very strongly in this painting.

come across
be communicated

Experts have attributed this painting to Joan Miró because of the distinctive style.

attribute to
believe that a certain person said or created something

It finally dawned on me that Claude was the killer.

dawn on
become clear to someone

It had never occurred to me that such a charming character could commit such a terrible crime.

occur to
suddenly come into someone's mind

39.3 THOUGHTS

While writing her memoir, Rebecca reflected on her childhood.

reflect on
carefully think about something

Before deciding whether or not to move to Canada, we need to think it through.

think through
considering the advantages and disadvantages of something

Selma is very creative. She thinks up lots of wonderful dishes.

think up
invent a new plan or idea in your mind

There's a lot to think about when buying a house, but it often boils down to money.

boil down to
be the most important reason

I asked Zoya if she'd like to work for us. She's thinking it over, and will let us know tomorrow.

think over
carefully think about a plan or idea before making a decision

The teacher asked us all to think of a famous person from history and write a story about them.

think of
create a mental image of something or someone

39.4 LISTEN TO THE AUDIO, THEN NUMBER THE PICTURES IN THE ORDER YOU HEAR THEM

A ☐

B 1

C ☐

D ☐

E ☐

F ☐

G ☐

H ☐

Aa 39.5 MATCH UP THE PAIRS OF SENTENCES THAT MEAN THE SAME THING

The president's speech touched on the economy, healthcare, and education. → The president's speech briefly mentioned the economy, healthcare, and education.

1. When my husband suggested buying a new kitchen, I ran with it.
2. When I told my friends I was starting my own business, they all got behind the idea.
3. They bombarded us with too much information during the training course.
4. Experts have attributed this painting to Joan Miró because of the distinctive style.
5. The artist's feelings of anger come across strongly in this painting.

- When I told my friends I was starting my own business, they all offered support.
- The president's speech briefly mentioned the economy, healthcare, and education.
- Experts believe that Joan Miró created this painting because of the distinctive style.
- When my husband suggested buying a new kitchen, I did what he suggested.
- The artist's feelings of anger are communicated strongly in this painting.
- They gave us too much information during the training course.

Aa 39.6 WRITE THE PHRASAL VERBS FROM THE PANEL IN THE CORRECT GROUPS

SEPARABLE	INSEPARABLE
____________	*run with*
____________	____________
____________	____________
____________	____________
____________	____________

come across   bounce off   come up with   put to   get behind   think through

~~run with~~   bombard with   touch on   think over

Aa 39.7 LOOK AT THE PICTURES AND COMPLETE THE SENTENCES USING PHRASAL VERBS

While writing her memoir, Rebecca *reflected on* her childhood.

1. The creative manager asked her team to ____________ as many ideas as they could.

2. It finally ____________ me that Claude was the killer.

3. We have ____________ three of the candidates. It's a choice between Danny and Carmen.

4. Ted has ____________ some good ideas for a new logo.

5. Selma is very creative. She ____________ lots of wonderful dishes.

40 Explaining things

See also:
fill in **37**

40.1 EXPLAINING THINGS

The politician alluded to housing in his speech, but mostly spoke about transportation.

allude to
mention something indirectly

How many times do I have to spell it out to you? You're not allowed to use your phone in class.

spell out
explain something very clearly (usually with anger or frustration)

During her speech, the senator kept coming back to her financial policies.

come back to
return to a subject

The interviewer asked me to expand on my experience of working with animals.

expand on
give more details about something

I asked the professor if he could go back over some of the points from the lecture.

go back over
explain the details of something again

Pete couldn't remember the French word for "swimming," so he acted it out.

act out
explain or show something by performing or re-enacting it

Yuri managed to put his ideas across very well during the debate.

put across
successfully explain an idea or express a feeling

My friend pointed out some of the mistakes I'd made in my code.

point out
help someone to notice something

Becky asked Sarah to fill her in on the latest gossip from the office.

fill (someone) in (on)
provide the latest or most important information about something

Gio didn't know anything about computers, so he asked the salesperson to dumb it down for him.

dumb down
make something easier to understand

40.2 LISTEN TO THE AUDIO AND MARK THE PHRASAL VERBS YOU HEAR

spell out ☑
allude to ☐

1 expand on ☐
point out ☐

2 act out ☐
dumb down ☐

3 come back to ☐
expand on ☐

4 fill in on ☐
point out ☐

5 put across ☐
go back over ☐

40.3 WRITE THE CORRECT PHRASAL VERB NEXT TO ITS DEFINITION, FILLING IN THE MISSING LETTERS

give more details about something = e x p a n d o n

1 successfully explain an idea or express a feeling = p _ _ a _ _ _ _ _

2 make something easier to understand = d _ _ _ d _ _ _

3 help someone to notice something = p _ _ _ _ o _ _

4 return to a subject = c _ _ _ b _ _ _ t _

5 mention something indirectly = a _ _ _ _ _ t _

6 explain the details of something again = g _ b _ _ _ o _ _ _

41 Truth and lies

41.1 TRUTH

I never caught on that Dad's company was in such debt.

catch on
realize something is happening

When it came out that he was bankrupt, I was shocked!

come out
become known

Conan finally owned up to breaking the window. He'd been denying it all morning.

own up (to)
admit that something was your fault

I have to level with you, Anu. The cake looks lovely, but it tastes terrible.

level with
tell someone the truth

41.2 LIES

We fell for the salesman's talk. The car we bought broke down after a few days.

fall for
be tricked into believing something

Pio's always making up excuses for handing in his homework late. Today, he claimed his school bag had been stolen.

make up
invent a story to explain something

Tyler has been promising to pay me back for months, but he's just stringing me along.

string along
give someone false hopes or make them believe something that is false

Alice accused me of messing her around when I canceled our date for a third time.

mess around
treat someone badly by deceiving them or changing plans regularly

After eating all the cake, John tried to cover it up by claiming the dog had eaten it.

cover up
hide the truth from other people

Larry's claim that he was at home on the night of the crime didn't add up.

add up
make sense, be a logical explanation

See also:
add up **14**, **25** come out **5**, **12** cover up **6** fall for **3** make out **52**
make up **44**, **52** mess around **21** put on **6**, **27**, **55**

It's really hard to suss the new neighbors out. They don't say anything about themselves.

suss out (UK)
understand what someone wants, or what kind of person they are

Gary was always exaggerating about how rich he was, but Safiya could see through his lies.

see through
be aware that something is not true

I've been trying to find out from Nisha who Sammy's dating.

find out
discover information

I think she knows more than she's letting on.

let on
admit or reveal something

Amrit promised his mother he'd stay home and study, but she caught him out when she heard him come home late.

catch out
discover that someone is lying

Mario glossed over the bad result, claiming the team would soon be back on form.

gloss over
try to make bad news or a mistake seem unimportant

Josie tried to explain away the damage to my car by saying it was just a small scratch.

explain away
try to persuade someone that a bad situation is not important or not your fault

Kirstie's been making out that everything's okay, but I know she's stressed about her interview.

make out
pretend

The CEO has been playing down the company's financial problems.

play down
make a problem seem unimportant

It looked as if Aaron had been injured, but I knew he was putting it on.

put on
pretend

Aa 41.3 MATCH THE DEFINITIONS TO THE CORRECT PHRASAL VERBS

	Definition	Phrasal verb
	discover that someone is lying → catch out	see through
1	be aware that something is not true	level with
2	try to make bad news or a mistake seem unimportant	catch out
3	hide the truth from other people	add up
4	make sense, be a logical explanation	cover up
5	be tricked into believing something	gloss over
6	invent a story to explain something	fall for
7	tell someone the truth	make up

41.4 LISTEN TO THE AUDIO AND MARK THE PHRASAL VERBS YOU HEAR

	suss out ☑	explain away ☐	see through ☐
1	play down ☐	make up ☐	make out ☐
2	cover up ☐	come out ☐	level with ☐
3	let on ☐	find out ☐	mess around ☐
4	gloss over ☐	string along ☐	add up ☐
5	put on ☐	catch out ☐	own up ☐
6	catch on ☐	explain away ☐	fall for ☐

Aa 41.5 LOOK AT THE PICTURES AND COMPLETE THE SENTENCES USING THE PHRASAL VERBS IN THE PANEL

I never ___caught on___ that Dad's company was in such debt.

1 I think she knows more than she's ______________ .

2 We ______________ the salesman's talk. The car we bought broke down after a few days.

3 When it ______________ that he was bankrupt, I was shocked!

4 Conan finally ______________ to breaking the window. He'd been denying it all morning.

5 The CEO has been ______________ the company's financial problems.

6 I've been trying to ______________ from Nisha who Sammy's dating.

7 Josie tried to ______________ the damage to my car by saying it was just a small scratch.

fell for	explain away	find out	letting on	owned up
came out	~~caught on~~	playing down		

42 Encouragement

42.1 ENCOURAGEMENT AND PERSUASION

The thought of winning first prize **spurred** Farukh **on**.

spur on
encourage someone, inspire someone to do something

Helen has **put** me **onto** this great new hair salon. I'm going to check it out.

put onto
tell someone about something they might find useful

When Zoe asked her daughter why she'd stolen the cookies, she said her elder brother had **put** her **up to** it.

put up to
encourage someone to do something that is wrong

Lisa's speech in favor of a new nature reserve has **brought** many people **around** to the idea.

bring around
persuade someone to support your idea

Kendra was very nervous, but was happy to see her friends **rooting for** her.

root for
show your support for someone

My son was upset, so I bought him an ice cream to **buck** him **up**.

buck up
make someone feel happier

Marcus's friends **egged** him **on** as he climbed the tree.

egg on
encourage someone to do something (often something naughty)

The crowd **urged** Mona **on** as she approached the end of the tightrope.

urge on
encourage someone to do something

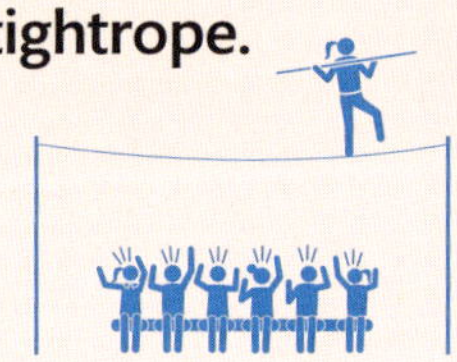

Rahul was skeptical about electric cars until the salesman **reasoned with** him.

reason with
offer logical arguments to try to change someone's mind

He eventually **won** him **over** by explaining how eco-friendly they are.

win over
successfully persuade someone to support your idea

Aa 42.2 MARK THE SENTENCES THAT ARE CORRECT

The thought of winning first prize spurred Farukh on. ☑
The thought of winning first prize spurred Farukh off. ☐

1. Helen has put me onto this great new hair salon. I'm going to check it out. ☐
   Helen has taken me onto this great new hair salon. I'm going to check it out. ☐

2. Lisa's speech in favor of a new nature reserve has brought many people around to the idea. ☐
   Lisa's speech in favor of a new nature reserve has brought many people about to the idea. ☐

3. Kendra was very nervous, but was happy to see her friends planting for her. ☐
   Kendra was very nervous, but was happy to see her friends rooting for her. ☐

4. Zoe's daughter said her elder brother had put her up to stealing the cookies. ☐
   Zoe's daughter said her elder brother had put her onto stealing the cookies. ☐

42.3 LISTEN TO THE AUDIO AND COMPLETE THE SENTENCES THAT DESCRIBE EACH PICTURE

Marcus's friends egged him on as he climbed the tree.

1. Kendra was very nervous, but was happy to see her friends ______________ her.

2. Rahul was skeptical about electric cars until the salesman ______________ him.

3. The crowd __________ Mona __________ as she approached the end of the tightrope.

4. He eventually __________ him __________ by explaining how eco-friendly they are.

5. My son was upset, so I bought him an ice cream to __________ him __________.

43 Agreeing and disagreeing

43.1 AGREEING AND DISAGREEING

Everyone agrees with John that Sian should get the job.

agree with
have the same opinion as someone

Martin and Simon disagreed with each other about what color to paint the kitchen.

disagree with
believe that someone or something is wrong

I want to go on an expensive vacation this year. I'm trying to persuade my husband to go along with the idea.

go along with
unwillingly agree to do something

My aunt frowns on people wearing shoes indoors. She makes her friends take them off when they visit.

frown on
disapprove of something

I can always count on my sister to comfort me when I'm upset.

count on
rely on someone

Laura objected to Ankita's proposals for the new restaurant.

object to
be opposed to something

During the debate, the politician hit out at her opponents.

hit out at
strongly criticize someone

Danny pulled Roberta up on her attitude towards the environment.

pull up on (UK)
criticize someone for a particular thing

Our local representative has come out against the plans for a new housing development.

come out against
reveal your opposition to something in public

Whenever there's a disagreement at work, Paulina always sides with our boss. It's so irritating!

side with
support someone in an argument

See also:
push back **16**

Carla **stood up to** the bullies. She told them to stop being mean to her brother.

stand up to
defend someone or yourself against someone else

The workers at the factory are **pushing back on** the management's attempt to introduce a pay cut.

push back (on)
resist or oppose something

I think Sonia **has** something **against** me. She never wants to talk to me.

have (something) against
dislike someone for an unknown reason

My idea was **shot down** by the panel before I had a chance to explain it to them.

shoot down
reject an idea

When Emily's boss accused her of being lazy, she **fought back** by showing him the clothes she had made that morning.

fight back
respond to someone who has criticized you

43.2 AVOIDING CONFLICT

Terry's colleagues always make fun of his shirts, but he just **laughs** it **off**.

laugh off
deal with criticism or a difficult situation by laughing at it

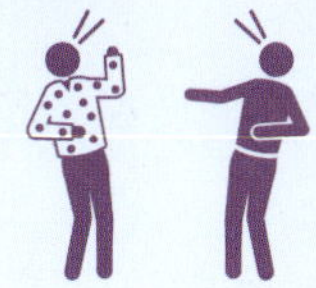

Donna bought her brother some chocolates to **make up for** the things she had said to him.

make up for
do something positive to correct a mistake

Paul usually **shrugs off** criticism of his cooking.

shrug off
treat something as if it is not important

The two companies have almost reached a deal. They just need to **iron out** a few last details.

iron out
solve small problems or details

Everyone criticized Magda's art when she started, but she **rose above** it and is a successful artist now.

rise above
not let criticism or a difficult situation affect you badly

Aa 43.3 MATCH THE PICTURES TO THE CORRECT SENTENCES

1 

2 

3 

4 

5 

I can count on my sister to comfort me when I'm upset.

Laura objected to Ankita's proposals for a new restaurant.

He pulled her up on her attitude towards the environment.

During the debate, she hit out at her opponents.

Paul usually shrugs off criticism of his cooking.

Carla stood up to the bullies and told them not to be mean.

43.4 LISTEN TO THE AUDIO AND MARK THE PHRASAL VERBS YOU HEAR

- A make up for ☐
- B fight back ☐
- C hit out at ☑
- D go along with ☐
- E shoot down ☐
- F iron out ☐
- G side with ☐
- H object to ☐
- I frown on ☐

Aa 43.5 CROSS OUT THE INCORRECT WORDS IN EACH SENTENCE

Paulina always sides ~~up~~ / **with** / ~~on~~ our boss. It's so irritating!

1. Everyone agrees **with** / **on** / **for** John that Sian should get the job.
2. Everyone criticized Magda's art, but she rose **above** / **for** / **on** it and is a successful artist now.
3. The workers are pushing **up for** / **back on** / **out of** the management's policies.
4. They disagreed **with** / **of** / **on** each other about what color to paint the kitchen.

Aa 43.6 READ THE STATEMENTS AND MARK THE CORRECT MEANING

Paul usually shrugs off criticism of his cooking.
- **Paul listens to criticism.** ☐
- **Paul doesn't listen to criticism.** ☑
- **Criticism helps Paul improve.** ☐

1. My aunt frowns on people wearing shoes indoors.
   - **My aunt disapproves.** ☐
   - **My aunt wears shoes indoors.** ☐
   - **My aunt doesn't wear shoes at all.** ☐

2. Paulina always sides with our boss.
   - **Paulina never supports our boss.** ☐
   - **Paulina doesn't like our boss.** ☐
   - **Paulina always supports our boss.** ☐

3. Laura objected to Ankita's proposals.
   - **Laura liked Ankita's proposals.** ☐
   - **Laura supported Ankita's proposals.** ☐
   - **Laura opposed Ankita's proposals.** ☐

4. Carla stood up to the bullies.
   - **Carla did not defend herself.** ☐
   - **Carla defended herself.** ☐
   - **Carla was one of the bullies.** ☐

5. They just need to iron out a few last details.
   - **They need to solve small problems.** ☐
   - **They need to create problems.** ☐
   - **They need to avoid problems.** ☐

Aa 43.7 REWRITE THE SENTENCES, CORRECTING THE ERRORS

My idea was **shot up** by the panel before I had a chance to explain it to them.

My idea was shot down by the panel before I had a chance to explain it to them.

1. I think Sonia **has** something **about** me. She never wants to talk to me.

2. Martin and Simon **disagreed on** each other about what color to paint the kitchen.

3. Our local representative has **come out under** the plans for a new housing development.

4. Donna bought her brother some chocolates to **make up by** the things she had said to him.

5. Terry's colleagues always make fun of his shirts, but he just **laughs** it **over**.

44 Opinions and arguments

44.1 OFFERING OPINIONS

Sorry, I'm not sure what you're getting at.

get at
imply, try to say something indirectly

The manager laid into the players after they lost another match.

lay into
criticize someone in an angry way

Anetta is always speaking out about environmental issues.

speak out
give your opinion publicly

Andy lashed out at someone who dropped litter in the street.

lash out (at)
criticize someone in an angry way

The professor weighed in on the debate about the new power station.

weigh in on
add your opinion to an ongoing discussion

Farah makes sure to base all her arguments on facts.

base on
use facts or arguments to support your opinion

44.2 JOINING ARGUMENTS

Only one of my colleagues stuck up for me when my boss criticized my work.

stick up for
defend someone or something

When Dad accused me of lying, Jo backed me up and told him I was telling the truth.

back up
give someone support by agreeing with them

Moira tried to drag Phil into her argument with the chef.

drag into
make someone join in an argument against their will

Phil, however, prefered to stay out of it.

stay out of
avoid becoming involved in an argument

See also:
back up **12** climb down **19** fall out **49**
make up **41**, **52** take back **10**, **16**

44.3 SURRENDERING, COMPROMISE, AND RECONCILIATION

Ben and Gus finally made up after their argument.

make up (with)
become friends again

They had fallen out when they both applied for the same job.

fall out (with)
have a disagreement with someone

Sam wanted his waiters to dress as hot dogs. He backed down when they threatened to quit.

back down
withdraw a demand or admit you were wrong

When Pete showed Martin the facts, Martin had to climb down and admit he was wrong.

climb down (UK)
admit you are wrong (after some resistance)

Kirsten had been threatening to fire Imran, but she backed off when he promised to work harder.

back off
withdraw a threat

Arun and Les patched things up after they had an argument.

patch up
sort out your differences and become friends again

I'm sorry I said I didn't like your dress, Katie. I take it back.

take back
admit that what you said was wrong

I'm trying to smooth things over with Anna, so I bought her some flowers.

smooth over (with)
resolve a problem or disagreement

Craig's parents finally caved in and bought him a games console.

cave in
agree to something (after a lot of resistance)

Ed hated Carla's new book, but he watered down his opinion when he wrote his review.

water down
make an opinion or proposal less strong

Aa 44.4 MATCH THE DEFINITIONS TO THE CORRECT PHRASAL VERBS

make someone join in an argument against their will → drag into	speak out
1 withdraw a threat	take back
2 give your opinion publicly	drag into
3 admit that what you said was wrong	stay out of
4 avoid becoming involved in an argument	base on
5 sort out your differences and become friends again	stick up for
6 use facts or arguments to support your opinion	back off
7 defend someone or something	patch up

44.5 LISTEN TO THE AUDIO, THEN NUMBER THE SENTENCES IN THE ORDER YOU HEAR THEM

A  Anetta is always speaking out about environmental issues. ☐

B  Arun and Les patched things up after they had an argument. ☐

C  Ed hated Carla's new book, but he watered down his opinion in his review. [1]

D  I'm sorry I said I didn't like your dress, Katie. I take it back. ☐

E  Farah makes sure to base all her arguments on facts. ☐

F  The professor weighed in on the debate about the new power station. ☐

Aa 44.6 WRITE THE PHRASAL VERBS FROM THE PANEL UNDER THE CORRECT DEFINITIONS

resolve a problem or disagreement

smooth over (with)

1. withdraw a threat

2. avoid becoming involved in an argument

3. give someone support by agreeing with them

4. defend someone or something

5. have a disagreement with someone

6. criticize someone in an angry way

7. withdraw a demand or admit you were wrong

back up	lash out (at)	stick up for	back off
back down	stay out of	~~smooth over (with)~~	fall out (with)

Aa 44.7 FILL IN THE GAPS USING THE WORDS IN THE PANEL TO CREATE PHRASAL VERBS

Ben and Gus finally [made *up*] after their argument.

1. When Pete showed Martin the facts, Martin had to [climb ____] and admit he was wrong.
2. The manager [laid ____] the players after they lost another match.
3. They had [fallen ____] when they both applied for the same job.
4. Craig's parents finally [caved ____] and bought him a games console.
5. Sorry, I'm not sure what you're [getting ____].

out	in	~~up~~	down	at	into

45 Emotions

45.1 POSITIVE EMOTIONS

The children burst out laughing when the clown pretended to fall over.

burst out
suddenly begin (laughing or crying)

Craig had had a bad day at work, but watching a funny movie cheered him up.

cheer up
become happier or make someone feel happier

Yana was upset, but she brightened up when I bought her some tickets to a concert.

brighten up
begin to feel happier

Anna hadn't been feeling great, but she perked up after a cup of tea and a cookie.

perk up
become happier or more lively

45.2 DEALING WITH EMOTIONS

When Linda feels stressed, she listens to music to help her calm down.

calm down
become calmer

I've been checking up on Andrei every day since he lost his job. He's been very upset.

check up on
check that someone is all right

I really feel for Kim. She's been so upset since her cat went missing.

feel for
feel sympathy toward someone

Petra's been sulking for days. I wish she'd snap out of it.

snap out of
suddenly improve your mood or behavior

Cory's daughter started to settle down as he sang her a soothing song.

settle down
become calmer

Jack's a very private person, but he finally opened up and told me how he feels.

open up
reveal your true feelings

See also:
brighten up **11** calm down **11** get over **32**, **53** move on **20**
open up **24** settle down **2** turn to **13**, **21**, **50** work through **20**

Sophie needs to lighten up. She's still studying even though it's her birthday today.

lighten up
stop taking everything so seriously

Patrick's love of music shines through when he starts playing his guitar.

shine through
be clear, easy to see (about a positive emotion or quality)

Hiro's jokes are hilarious. He really cracks me up.

crack up
begin laughing or make someone laugh a lot

Donny's face lit up when he saw the presents waiting for him on the table.

light up
suddenly look happy

Kathy and Jamal broke up last month, but Kathy is still finding it hard to get over it.

get over
recover from a bad experience

Kathy is finally moving on after her break up with Jamal last year.

move on
stop thinking about someone or something

Ed's really toughened up after three years in the army.

toughen up
become physically or mentally stronger

Whenever I'm upset, I know I can turn to my sister.

turn to
ask someone for help

I see a therapist to help me work through my problems.

work through
deal with your problems in a systematic way

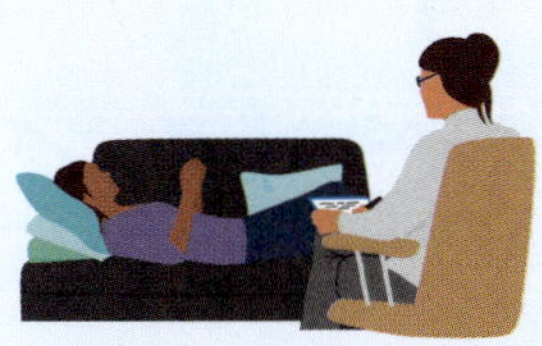

My therapist has helped me to cope with many of my problems.

cope with
manage, deal with a situation

45.3 READ THE STATEMENTS AND MARK THE CORRECT MEANING

The children burst out laughing.

They suddenly stopped laughing. ☐
They suddenly began laughing. ☑
They did not laugh. ☐

1 Ed's toughened up after joining the army.

Ed's become stronger. ☐
Ed's become weaker. ☐
Ed's not tough enough. ☐

2 She has helped me cope with my problems.

She has helped me create problems. ☐
She has helped me manage my problems. ☐
She has created problems for me. ☐

3 Kathy is trying to get over her breakup.

Kathy is trying to recover from it. ☐
Kathy is breaking up with someone. ☐
Kathy has forgotten her breakup. ☐

4 Anna perked up after a cup of tea.

Anna fell asleep. ☐
Anna became lazy. ☐
Anna became happier. ☐

45.4 LISTEN TO THE AUDIO AND MATCH THE IMAGES TO THE CORRECT PHRASAL VERBS

1 

2 

3 

4 

5 

burst out

settle down

shine through

light up

crack up

work through

45.5 CROSS OUT THE INCORRECT WORDS IN EACH SENTENCE

I see a therapist to help me work ~~under~~ / through / ~~over~~ my problems.

1 Donny's face lit up / out / off when he saw the presents waiting for him on the table.

2 Jack's a very private person, but he finally opened on / up / in and told me how he feels.

3 When Linda feels stressed, she listens to music to help her calm up / down / out.

4 The children burst off / in / out laughing when the clown pretended to fall over.

Aa 45.6 FILL IN THE GAPS, PUTTING THE WORDS IN THE CORRECT ORDER

down | settle | to

Cory's daughter started *to* *settle* *down* as he sang her a soothing song.

up | on | checking

1. I've been ________ ________ ________ Andrei every day since he lost his job.

up | cheered | him

2. Craig had had a bad day at work, but watching a funny movie ________ ________ ________.

up | me | cracks

3. Hiro's jokes are hilarious. He really ________ ________ ________.

when | brightened | up

4. Yana was upset, but she ________ ________ ________ I bought her tickets to a concert.

Aa 45.7 REWRITE THE SENTENCES, CORRECTING THE ERRORS

Whenever I'm upset, I know I can **turn around** my sister.

Whenever I'm upset, I know I can turn to my sister.

1. Sophie needs to **lighten down**. She's still studying even though it's her birthday today.

____

2. I really **feel about** Kim. She's been so upset since her cat went missing.

____

3. Kathy is finally **moving off** after her breakup with Jamal last year.

____

4. Petra's been sulking for days. I wish she'd **snap in of** it.

____

46 Negative emotions

46.1 NEGATIVE EMOTIONS

Chris had been bottling up his emotions for a long time.

bottle up
feel unable to show your emotions to others

He eventually broke down and admitted that he was really upset.

break down
start to cry

Andy fell apart when I told him that I was moving to another country.

fall apart
become very emotional, lose control

This song is so moving. It always sets me off.

set off
make someone start crying

It really gets to me when people leave their trash on the metro.

get to
irritate or upset someone

Tamal and Sam choked up when the hero died at the end of the movie.

choke up
become emotional or upset

I'm sick of my neighbors arguing. It's been getting me down for months.

get down
make someone feel depressed

Bella welled up when Pete asked her to marry him.

well up
have your eyes fill with tears, start to cry

Stop taking it out on me. It's not my fault the weather is awful.

take out on
behave in a bad way to someone even though it is not their fault

When Lisa walked onto the stage she froze up. She couldn't say anything!

freeze up
suddenly become unable to communicate

See also:
break down **9**, **50** fall apart **49** get down **19**, **53**
get to **53** set off **35**, **53**

Sadie's anger about her boss's rude behavior had been building up.

build up
become bigger or stronger

It eventually spilled over, and Sadie told her how she felt.

spill over
start to show (in an uncontrollable way)

Simone's eyes misted over as she told me about her childhood in the countryside.

mist over
(about eyes) fill with tears

Clare flew into a rage when her computer crashed and lost all her work.

fly into
(about temper, rage, or panic) suddenly become very angry or scared

My husband tenses up whenever I try to talk about money with him.

tense up
suddenly become tense or anxious

Troy freaked out when he noticed the enormous spider climbing up the wall.

freak out
become very upset or afraid (informal)

My grandchildren love to wind me up. They're always playing tricks on me.

wind up
tease someone, make someone angry

Work has been weighing on me a lot recently.

weigh on
make someone feel worried or unhappy

My manager is usually very understanding, but he blew up when I told him that I'd left my work laptop on the train.

blow up
suddenly become very angry

46.2 MATCH THE BEGINNINGS OF THE SENTENCES TO THE CORRECT ENDINGS

It really gets to me when → people leave their trash on the metro.

1. My husband tenses up whenever
2. This song is so moving.
3. Troy freaked out when he noticed
4. Clare flew into a rage when
5. Stop taking it out on me.
6. My grandchildren love to wind me up.

- I try to talk about money with him.
- her computer crashed and lost all her work.
- They're always playing tricks on me.
- people leave their trash on the metro.
- the enormous spider climbing up the wall.
- It always sets me off.
- It's not my fault the weather is awful.

46.3 LISTEN TO THE AUDIO AND COMPLETE THE SENTENCES THAT DESCRIBE EACH PICTURE

Simone's eyes *misted over* as she told me about her childhood in the countryside.

1. Sadie's anger about her boss's rude behavior had been ______________ .

2. Tamal and Sam ______________ when the hero died at the end of the movie.

3. When Lisa walked onto the stage she ______________ . She couldn't say anything!

4. He eventually ______________ and admitted that he was really upset.

5. My manager ______________ when I told him that I'd left my work laptop on the train.

Aa 46.4 LOOK AT THE PICTURES AND COMPLETE THE SENTENCES USING THE PHRASAL VERBS IN THE PANEL

Andy ___fell apart___ when I told him that I was moving to another country.

1. Bella ______________ when Pete asked her to marry him.

2. It eventually ______________ , and Sadie told her how she felt.

3. Chris had been ______________ his emotions for a long time.

4. Work has been ______________ me a lot recently.

5. Clare ______________ a rage when her computer crashed and lost all her work.

spilled over	flew into	~~fell apart~~	bottling up	welled up	weighing on

Aa 46.5 WRITE THE CORRECT PHRASAL VERB NEXT TO ITS DEFINITION, FILLING IN THE MISSING LETTERS

make someone start crying = s e t o f f

1. make someone feel depressed = g _ _ d _ _ _
2. tease someone, make someone angry = w _ _ _ u _
3. start to cry = b _ _ _ _ d _ _ _
4. suddenly become very angry = b _ _ _ u _

47 Making decisions

47.1 MAKING DECISIONS

Lisa found it hard to choose a dress, but eventually decided on the red one.

decide on
reach a decision

After a lot of thought, Rob went for the fish instead of the steak.

go for
choose

Moving to New Zealand next year hinges on us saving enough money.

hinge on
depend completely on something

It's so hard to choose! I'm leaning toward the red sports car.

lean toward
be more likely to choose one option than another

Marie didn't know which new job to accept, so she decided to sleep on it.

sleep on
wait until the next day before making a decision

Shona regrets her decision to quit, but she's going to have to live with it.

live with
accept an unpleasant decision or situation

We loved your plans for the new apartment block. But our decision came down to funding.

come down to
depend on one point

After so many failures, Stephen's banking on this new recipe to impress his guests.

bank on
depend on

We were sure our café would be a success, but forgot to factor in the local competition.

factor in
take into consideration

See also:
arrive at **35** go for **54** live with **2**

settle on
choose (after thinking about or discussing it)

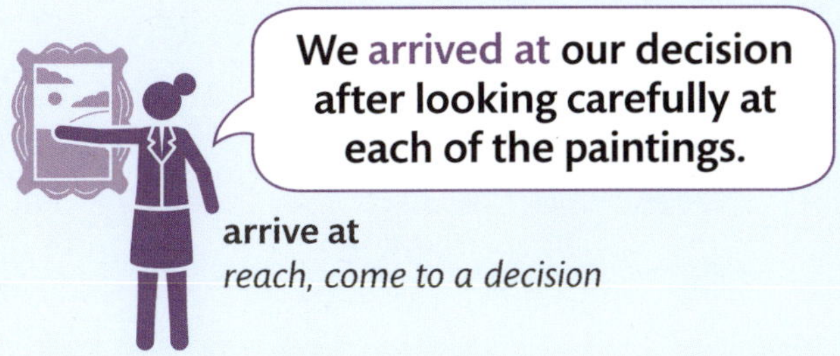

arrive at
reach, come to a decision

The workers wanted a 5% pay raise, but eventually settled for 3%.

settle for
agree to something although it is not what you first wanted

Yasmin has been toying with the idea of getting her hair cut short, but has never done it.

toy with
consider, play with an idea

Paula weighed up her options before deciding which camera to buy.

weigh up
consider positive and negative things before making a decision

Somrita has been mulling over which candidate to hire.

mull over
think about something for some time before making a decision

Ahmed's betting on it being a hot summer this year so he's bought an ice-cream van.

bet on
act on a hope or prediction

We have narrowed down our list of potential homes to two properties.

narrow down
reduce the number of choices

Sonia opted out of the boat trip. She always gets sea sick.

opt out (of)
choose not to do something

Archie picked out the toy he wanted for his birthday.

pick out
choose carefully from a group

Aa 47.2 CROSS OUT THE INCORRECT WORDS IN EACH SENTENCE

Somrita has been mulling ~~in~~ / **over** / ~~on~~ which candidate to hire.

1  Sonia opted **over** / **on** / **out** of the boat trip. She always gets sea sick.

2  Yasmin has been toying **on** / **with** / **to** the idea of getting her hair cut short.

3  The workers wanted a 5% pay raise, but settled **out** / **for** / **in** 3%.

4  Shona regrets her decision to quit, but she's going to have to live **with** / **in** / **on** it.

5  After a lot of thought, Rob went **on** / **out** / **for** the fish instead of the steak.

Aa 47.3 MATCH THE DEFINITIONS TO THE CORRECT PHRASAL VERBS

	depend completely on something	→ hinge on	decide on
1	reach a decision		opt out
2	take into consideration		hinge on
3	think about something before making a decision		pick out
4	choose carefully from a group		factor in
5	choose not to do something		lean toward
6	be more likely to choose one option than another		mull over

47.4 LISTEN TO THE AUDIO AND MARK THE PHRASAL VERBS YOU HEAR

bet on ☑
bet in ☐

1 weigh up ☐
weigh out ☐

2 narrow down ☐
narrow up ☐

3 pick over ☐
pick out ☐

4 sleep on ☐
sleep in ☐

5 lean toward ☐
lean on ☐

47.5 FILL IN THE GAPS, PUTTING THE WORDS IN THE CORRECT ORDER

up | weighed | her

Paula *weighed* *up* *her* options before deciding which camera to buy.

on | us | hinges

1 Moving to New Zealand next year ______ ______ ______ saving enough money.

on | settled | a

2 Can you tell us how you ______ ______ ______ winner?

decided | the | on

3 Lisa found it hard to choose a dress, but eventually ______ ______ ______ red one.

this | on | banking

4 Stephen is ______ ______ ______ new recipe to impress his guests.

48 Making mistakes

48.1 MAKING MISTAKES

Coralie's graph didn't make sense, so she looked through the data again to see where she'd slipped up.

slip up
make a mistake

Wang thought he'd bought everyone a drink until he noticed he'd missed Ellie out.

miss out
forget to include someone or something in an activity

When Juan missed the penalty, his teammates rubbed it in by laughing at him.

rub in
make someone feel worse about a mistake or failure

I was relying on Selma to bring candles for the cake, but she let me down.

let down
fail to meet someone's expectations or fail to keep a promise

The spelling mistake in Juanita's homework jumped out at me.

jump out at
be obvious to someone

I'll never live down the time I dropped Erin's birthday cake in the middle of her party.

live down
have people forget about an embarrassing mistake you made

Tariq landed himself in trouble when he forgot to do his homework.

land in
get into a bad situation

When Chris got home from work, he realized that he had mixed his bag up with Simon's.

mix up (with)
accidentally mistake one thing for something else

Enzo went back to the café when he realized he'd left his wallet behind.

leave behind
forget to take someone or something with you

I crossed out the misspelled word and wrote it again correctly.

cross out
draw a line or lines through a word

48.2 LISTEN TO THE AUDIO, THEN NUMBER THE SENTENCES IN THE ORDER YOU HEAR THEM

A  Enzo went back to the café when he realized he'd left his wallet behind. ☐

B  Tariq landed himself in trouble when he forgot to do his homework. ☐

C  When Juan missed the penalty, his teammates rubbed it in by laughing at him. [1]

D  I crossed out the misspelled word and wrote it again correctly. ☐

E  The spelling mistake in Juanita's homework jumped out at me. ☐

Aa 48.3 REWRITE THE SENTENCES, CORRECTING THE ERRORS

Jimish thought he'd bought everyone a drink until he noticed he'd **missed** Ellie **on**.

Jimish thought he'd bought everyone a drink until he noticed he'd missed Ellie out.

1. I was relying on Selma to bring candles for the cake, but she **letting** me **down**.

____

2. I'll never **die down** the time I dropped Erin's birthday cake in the middle of her party.

____

3. Coralie's graph didn't make sense, so she looked through the data again to see where she'd **slipping up**.

____

4. When Chris got home from work, he realized that he had **mixed** his bag **up for** Simon's.

____

5. The spelling mistake in Juanita's homework **pounced out at** me.

____

49 Accidents and damage

49.1 ACCIDENTS

Chrissy accidentally **broke** the handle **off** the antique vase.

break off
remove by force

The hairdresser has completely **messed up** Kira's hair. She's furious about it.

mess up
make something untidy or unattractive, do something incorrectly

The old book **came apart** in the librarian's hands.

come apart
fall to pieces

I **banged into** the door while leaving the house.

bang into
hit someone or something by mistake

The dog **knocked over** the plant pot as it chased the cat.

knock over
hit something and make it fall to the ground

Takira **tripped over** one of her son's toys.

trip over
hit something with your foot and fall to the ground as a result

49.3 PHRASAL VERBS WITH "FALL"

When Omar **fell over** in the backyard, his dad rushed over to help him.

fall over
fall to the ground from a standing position

Rodrigo slammed the door so hard that the pictures **fell off** the wall.

fall off
fall to the ground from a higher point or surface

The old manor house Andrei wants to buy looks as if it's about to **fall down**.

fall down
be in a very bad state, fall to the ground (about a building)

See also:
break off **30** fall apart **46**
fall out **44** wear out **33**

49.2 DAMAGE

When I got home, I found that the dog had torn a cushion apart.

tear apart
destroy by tearing into pieces

After her favorite band split up, Jo tore up all her posters of them.

tear up
break something into pieces by ripping it

Colin accidentally drove into a tree and smashed up his van.

smash up
break something into pieces

The drain was clogged up with old leaves, so I had to unblock it.

clog up
become blocked

My son has worn out another pair of shoes!

wear out
use something so much that it cannot be used anymore

Jorge took the old clock apart to fix it.

take apart
disassemble something, separate it into its parts

Sanjay's old car is falling apart. He's had it since he was a teenager.

fall apart
break into pieces (because of age or bad quality)

David's wallet fell out of his pocket while he was running for the bus.

fall out (of)
fall from an enclosed place

After the leak in the room above, it looked like the ceiling might fall in.

fall in
crumble and fall to the ground

Aa 49.4 MARK THE SENTENCES THAT ARE CORRECT

My son has worn out another pair of shoes! ☑
My son has worn off another pair of shoes! ☐

1. After the leak in the room above, it looked like the ceiling might fall in. ☐
   After the leak in the room above, it looked like the ceiling might fall on. ☐

2. The dog knocked out the plant pot as it chased the cat. ☐
   The dog knocked over the plant pot as it chased the cat. ☐

3. Jorge took the old clock under to fix it. ☐
   Jorge took the old clock apart to fix it. ☐

4. When I got home, I found that the dog had torn a cushion apart. ☐
   When I got home, I found that the dog had torn a cushion aside. ☐

49.5 LISTEN TO THE AUDIO, THEN NUMBER THE PICTURES IN THE ORDER YOU HEAR THEM

A ☐

B 1

C ☐

D ☐

E ☐

F ☐

Aa 49.6 MATCH THE VERBS TO THE CORRECT PARTICLES TO MAKE PHRASAL VERBS

	clog	out
1	smash	over
2	wear	up
3	bang	off
4	trip	up
5	fall	into
6	break	in

Aa 49.7 LOOK AT THE PICTURES AND COMPLETE THE SENTENCES USING THE PHRASAL VERBS IN THE PANEL

David's wallet ___*fell out of*___ his pocket while he was running for the bus.

4 The old book ________________ in the librarian's hands.

1 I ________________ the door while leaving the house.

5 The drain was ________________ with old leaves, so I had to unblock it.

2 Colin accidentally drove into a tree and ________________ his van.

6 Sanjay's old car is ________________. He's had it since he was a teenager.

3 Rodrigo slammed the door so hard that the pictures ________________ the wall.

7 The old manor house Andrei wants to buy looks as if it's about to ________________.

came apart	fall down	fell off	banged into
falling apart	~~fell out of~~	smashed up	clogged up

50 Problems and solutions

50.1 PROBLEMS AND SOLUTIONS

Sorry, I'll be home late tonight. Something's come up.

come up
happen unexpectedly

The proposals for a new highway have come up against a lot of local opposition.

come up against
encounter difficulties

It was very hard for Somrita and her friends to relax with their final exams hanging over them.

hang over
be a source of worry

While climbing the mountain, we had to contend with strong winds and heavy rain.

contend with
deal with difficulties or opposition

A number of problems have cropped up with the new printer. We need to get someone to fix it.

crop up
happen (often unexpectedly)

Writing your thesis is easier if you break it down into small sections.

break down
make something easier to understand by separating it into smaller parts

I thought the event was going to be a disaster, but it turned out alright.

turn out
happen differently than expected

Owen is great with customers. He deals with their complaints fairly, and never loses his temper.

deal with
manage or solve a problem

Ben and I cleared up our disagreement when we realized it was all just a misunderstanding.

clear up
solve a problem, resolve an argument

Bitna told Danny she was nervous about her presentation, but he just brushed it aside.

brush aside
treat a problem as unimportant, refuse to take it seriously

See also: break down **9**, **46** call in **4**, **22** check out **10**, **35** clear up **11**, **32** come up **16**, **36**, **52** get around **35**, **53** think through **39** turn to **13**, **21**, **45**

Clare and Wei Ting had to sort out a problem with their experiment.

sort out
find a solution to a problem

They stayed up late to thrash it out and find a solution.

thrash out
discuss a problem to find a solution

Sawad's computer crashed, but she worked around it by using pen and paper instead.

work around
avoid an obstacle that is stopping you from achieving something

Kavitha didn't know why her equation was wrong, so she thought it through carefully.

think through
consider something methodically

Anton had run out of green paint, but he managed to get around it.

get around
avoid or solve a problem or obstacle

It's taken me all evening to figure out how to turn on this new television.

figure out
find a solution to a problem

Femmy's thinking of moving to a new part of town, so she went to check out the area.

check out
find out if someone or something is acceptable

One of the pipes was leaking, so we called in a plumber to fix it.

call in
ask a skilled person to deal with a problem for you

Whenever Gitanjali has a problem, she turns to her grandmother for advice.

turn to
go to someone for help or advice

50.2 LISTEN TO THE AUDIO, THEN NUMBER THE PICTURES IN THE ORDER YOU HEAR THEM

A ☐

B 1

C ☐

D ☐

E ☐

F ☐

G ☐

H ☐

50.3 MATCH UP THE PAIRS OF SENTENCES THAT MEAN THE SAME THING

Clare and Wei Ting had to sort out a problem with their experiment. → Clare and Wei Ting had to find a solution to a problem with their experiment.

1. Whenever Gitanjali has a problem, she turns to her grandmother for advice.
2. While climbing the mountain, we had to contend with strong winds and heavy rain.
3. The proposals for a new highway have come up against a lot of local opposition.
4. One of the pipes was leaking, so we called in a plumber to fix it.
5. Writing your thesis is easier if you break it down into small sections.
6. It's taken me all evening to figure out how to turn on this new television.

- While climbing the mountain, we had to deal with strong winds and heavy rain.
- Clare and Wei Ting had to find a solution to a problem with their experiment.
- It's taken me all evening to find out how to turn on this new television.
- One of the pipes was leaking, so we asked a plumber to fix it.
- Whenever Gitanjali has a problem, she goes to her grandmother for advice.
- The proposals for a new highway have encountered a lot of local opposition.
- Writing your thesis is easier if you separate it into small sections.

Aa 50.4 WRITE THE PHRASAL VERBS FROM THE PANEL IN THE CORRECT GROUPS

SEPARABLE	INSEPARABLE
	turn to

come up against · break down · crop up · thrash out · brush aside · get around · think through · ~~turn to~~

Aa 50.5 WRITE THE PHRASAL VERBS FROM THE PANEL UNDER THE CORRECT DEFINITIONS

avoid or solve a problem or obstacle

get around

4 solve a problem, resolve an argument

1 happen differently than expected

5 treat a problem as unimportant, refuse to take it seriously

2 consider something methodically

6 ask a skilled person to deal with a problem for you

3 find a solution to a problem

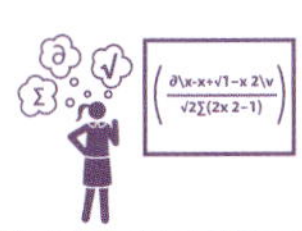

7 find out if someone or something is acceptable

sort out · check out · think through · brush aside · turn out · ~~get around~~ · clear up · thrash out

51 Secrets and surprises

51.1 SECRETS

Jessica has been keeping the name of her new boyfriend from me.

keep from
not tell someone something

Paolo has prepared a new sculpture for the exhibition. I've asked him what it is, but he's not giving anything away!

give away
reveal a secret

I only cottoned onto the fact that Lisa and Pete were dating when I saw them at the ice rink together.

cotton on(to) (UK)
begin to understand or realize something

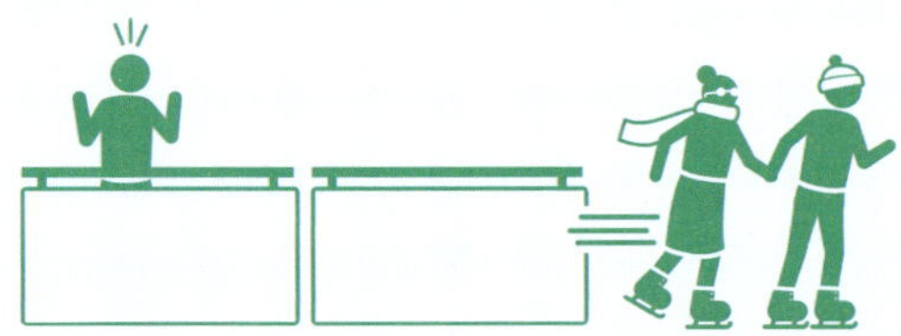

51.2 SURPRISES

We were all eating our dinner when the dog burst into the room.

burst in(to)
enter a room or building suddenly

I was bowled over when Nadia announced that she had been accepted into dance school.

bowl over
amaze or impress someone

Kamal was blown away by Jose's account of his adventures in the Amazon.

blow away
impress very strongly (informal)

Mollie crept up on her grandfather while he slept in the garden.

creep up on
approach someone quietly to surprise them

My best friend sprang it on me last night that she's moving to Canada.

spring on
announce something without warning

The surprising news was a lot to take in.

take in
understand or accept some news or information

See also:
blurt out **36** creep up on **15** give away **55**
keep from **33** slip out **5** take in **6**, **55**

My little sister blurted out to Dad that we'd organized a surprise party for him. She can't keep a secret.

blurt out
say something suddenly, without thinking about it

I didn't mean to tell the team that it was your birthday. It just slipped out.

slip out
say something by mistake

The movie star tried to hush up the fact that she had a new boyfriend.

hush up
conceal the truth

Clara can't believe she passed her medical exams. It's going to take a while for it to sink in.

sink in
be fully understood

My daughter often pretends to be a dinosaur. We all have to play along with her.

play along
pretend something is true or that you believe in something

People have woken up to the fact that we need to look after the environment.

wake up to
realize the importance of something

While I was on vacation in Venice, I bumped into one of my cousins. I couldn't believe it.

bump into
meet someone without expecting it

I was shopping at the antiques market when I stumbled upon a valuable necklace.

stumble upon
find by chance

I was taken aback when Tia and Juan told me they were getting married.

take aback
surprisee or shock someone

Aa 51.3 MATCH THE BEGINNINGS OF THE SENTENCES TO THE CORRECT ENDINGS

Kamal was blown away by Jose's → account of his adventures in the Amazon.

1. I didn't mean to tell the team
2. The movie star tried to hush up
3. Jessica has been keeping
4. I was bowled over when Nadia announced
5. Mollie crept up on her grandfather

- that it was your birthday. It just slipped out.
- that she had been accepted into dance school.
- account of his adventures in the Amazon.
- while he slept in the garden.
- the fact that she had a new boyfriend.
- the name of her new boyfriend from me.

Aa 51.4 CROSS OUT THE INCORRECT WORDS IN EACH SENTENCE

We were all eating our dinner when the dog burst ~~onto~~ / into / ~~through~~ the room.

1.  Clara can't believe she passed her exams. It's going to take a while for it to sink **down** / **of** / **in**.

2.  People have woken **for** / **up** / **of** to the fact that we need to look after the environment.

3.  I was shopping at the antiques market when I stumbled **over** / **upon** / **in** a valuable necklace.

4.  My best friend **sprang** / **jumped** / **splashed** it on me last night that she's moving to Canada.

5.  I was taken **about** / **aback** / **around** when Tia and Juan told me they were getting married.

51.5 LISTEN TO THE AUDIO AND MATCH THE IMAGES TO THE CORRECT PHRASAL VERBS

1 

2 

3 

4 

play along

blurt out

cotton onto

give away

bump into

51.6 REWRITE THE SENTENCES, PUTTING THE WORDS IN THE CORRECT ORDER

surprising | lot | was | The | to | take | in. | news | a

The surprising news was a lot to take in.

a | the | stumbled | valuable | market. | I | necklace | upon | at | antiques

1 ______________________________

keeping | Jessica | the | me. | new | has | name | boyfriend | her | been | of | from

2 ______________________________

on | grandfather | crept | her | up | in | slept | he | the | Mollie | while | garden.

3 ______________________________

room. | the | We | our | were | dinner | burst | into | eating | when | dog | the

4 ______________________________

52 "Come," "make," and "do"

52.1 PHRASAL VERBS WITH "COME"

Hetty's career as a musician came about after a producer saw her performing.

come about
happen (often without planning)

When I tried to log into my account, a message came up saying that my account had been blocked.

come up
appear (on screen)

Staying in touch with friends became much easier once the internet came along.

come along
appear, become available, start to exist

Ben and Eleanor came out of the toy store with presents for their grandchildren.

come out (of)
leave a room, building, or enclosed space

Natsuo came across the room to speak to us.

come across
move across a room, space, country, etc.

The company has come under attack for its high carbon emissions.

come under
experience something negative (such as criticism, threat, or attack)

Derek sat down in front of the TV when the ten o'clock news came on.

come on
start (about a TV program)

My daughter's still waiting for her results to come through. She's so nervous.

come through
arrive (about news or information)

No matter how much we clean it, this graffiti won't come off the wall.

come off
be removed

See also: come across **1**, **39** come along **5**, **31** come off **6**, **26** come on **27**, **56** come out (of) **6** come up **16**, **36**, **50** do up **52** make for **37** make out **41** make up **41**, **44**

52.2 PHRASAL VERBS WITH "MAKE"

Lots of talented people make up our circus's team of acrobats.

make up
constitute, form something

Luanne struggled to make out what the train conductor was saying.

make out
manage to see, hear, or understand

We were about to eat dinner when the dog made off with the leg of lamb.

make off with
escape with something

With hot weather expected, thousands of tourists made for the coast.

make for
go toward a place

When I asked Kim what she made of Toshi's new novel, she said she loved it.

make of
have an opinion of something

52.3 PHRASAL VERBS WITH "DO"

Emily is doing up her house at the moment. It's going to look great when she's finished.

do up
improve, renovate

With so many people using bank cards, we may be able to do away with cash in the future.

do away with
abolish, no longer need or use

The council needs to decide what it's going to do about the city's litter problem.

do about
do something to solve a problem

Riya was very disappointed with her wedding cake, and insisted it be done over.

do over (US)
do something again

Aa 52.4 MATCH THE PHRASAL VERBS TO THE CORRECT DEFINITIONS

	Phrasal verb	Definition
	do up → improve, renovate	be removed
1	come off	have an opinion of something
2	come up	improve, renovate
3	do about	appear (on screen)
4	make of	escape with something
5	make for	abolish, no longer need or use
6	make off with	go toward a place
7	do away with	do something to solve a problem

52.5 LISTEN TO THE AUDIO, THEN NUMBER THE SENTENCES IN THE ORDER YOU HEAR THEM

A  Natsuo came across the room to speak to us. ☐

B  We were about to eat dinner when the dog made off with the leg of lamb. ☐

C  Ben and Eleanor came out of the toy store with presents for their grandchildren. [1]

D  My daughter's still waiting for her results to come through. She's so nervous. ☐

E  When I asked Kim what she made of Toshi's new novel, she said she loved it. ☐

F  Staying in touch with friends became much easier once the internet came along. ☐

Aa 52.6 FILL IN THE GAPS USING THE PHRASAL VERBS IN THE PANEL

The company has *come under* attack for its high carbon emissions.

1. Riya was disappointed with her wedding cake, and insisted it be ________________ .
2. With hot weather expected, thousands of tourists ________________ the coast.
3. Lots of talented people ________________ our circus's team of acrobats.
4. Natsuo ________________ the room to speak to us.
5. The council has to decide what it's going to ________________ the litter problem.
6. Luanne struggled to ________________ what the train conductor was saying.
7. No matter how much we clean it, this graffiti won't ________________ the wall.

do about
came across
made for
~~come under~~
make out
make up
come off
done over

Aa 52.7 LOOK AT THE PICTURES AND COMPLETE THE SENTENCES USING PHRASAL VERBS

Emily is *doing up* her house at the moment. It's going to look great when she's finished.

1. Hetty's career as a musician ________________ after a producer saw her performing.

2. Derek sat down in front of the TV when the ten o'clock news ________________ .

3. Luanne struggled to ________________ what the train conductor was saying.

4. When I tried to log in, a message ________________ saying that my account had been blocked.

5. Lots of talented people ________________ our circus's team of acrobats.

53 "Get" and "set"

53.1 PHRASAL VERBS WITH "GET"

Claude got up from his chair and went to make some more tea.

get up (from)
stand up (from sitting)

Let's just clean the kitchen now and get it over with.

get over with
complete a task you don't want to do

It's almost eleven o'clock. We should get down to work.

get down to
start to focus on a task

Can you help me get the shopping in, please?

get in
bring something inside

Chad's oven had broken, but he got around it by using the microwave instead.

get around
avoid an obstacle, deal with a problem

Cheryl's dog keeps getting over the fence into the neighbor's backyard.

get over
find a way over an obstacle

53.2 PHRASAL VERBS WITH "SET"

Harry burned the dinner and set off the smoke detector.

set off
activate, cause something to start happening

As Martin walked home late at night, fear began to set in.

set in
begin (about something unpleasant that may last a long time)

The bad weather has set us back by two weeks. We won't finish building the bridge until November.

set back
cost time, money, or progress

See also: get around **35**, **50** get down **19**, **46** get in **8**, **9** get out **9**, **56** get over **32**, **45** get to **46** get together **5** get up **8** set off **35**, **46** set out **23**, **35** set up **3**, **12**

Lee got his fishing rod out of the garage and carried it to his car.

get out (of)
remove something (from a bag, box, room, etc.)

Ramona always gets her message across, even when she's explaining complicated scientific theories.

get across
communicate a message successfully

Glen climbed the ladder to get the cat down from the tree.

get down (from)
retrieve something from a higher position

Before accusing Simon, the police had to get their facts together.

get together
organize information or belongings

As soon as we got to the ski resort, we went straight to the slopes.

get to
arrive at

After Gia was rude to me, I got back at her by not inviting her to my wedding.

get back at
get revenge on somebody

Lee's speed sets him apart from the other players in the tournament.

set apart (from)
make someone or something special in comparison to others

The security guard threatened to set his dog on us if we didn't leave immediately.

set on
order someone or something to attack someone

After leaving school, Romesh set up his own business selling surfboards.

set up
start (a business)

Mary set out all her qualifications and experience in her resume.

set out
explain information in detail

53.3 LISTEN TO THE AUDIO AND COMPLETE THE SENTENCES THAT DESCRIBE EACH PICTURE

Claude got up from his chair and went to make some more tea.

1 Cheryl's dog keeps ______ the fence into the neighbor's backyard.

2 Harry burned the dinner and ______ the smoke detector.

3 As Martin walked home late at night, fear began to ______ .

4 It's almost eleven o'clock. We should ______ work.

5 Mary ______ all her qualifications and experience in her resume.

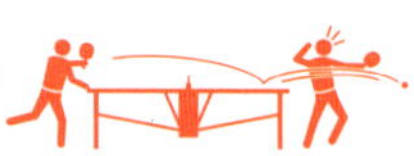

6 Lee's speed ______ the other players in the tournament.

53.4 WRITE THE PHRASAL VERBS FROM THE PANEL IN THE CORRECT GROUPS

SEPARABLE	INSEPARABLE
	get around

get up (from) set back get to set on ~~get around~~ get across set in get together

Aa 53.5 MATCH THE DEFINITIONS TO THE CORRECT PHRASAL VERBS

avoid an obstacle, deal with a problem → get around

1. order someone or something to attack someone
2. arrive at
3. cost time, money, or progress
4. get revenge on somebody
5. communicate a message successfully
6. organize information or belongings
7. start (a business)

- get to
- get across
- get around
- set on
- get together
- set back
- set up
- get back at

Aa 53.6 REWRITE THE SENTENCES, CORRECTING THE ERRORS

Let's just clean the kitchen now and **set** it **over with**.

Let's just clean the kitchen now and get it over with.

1. Lee **got** his fishing rod **up of** the garage and carried it to his car.

2. The security guard threatened to **get** his dog **on** us if we didn't leave immediately.

3. Can you help me **got** the shopping **in**, please?

4. Before accusing Simon, the police had to **get** their facts **up**.

5. As soon as we **gotten to** the ski resort, we went straight to the slopes.

54 "Go"

54.1 PHRASAL VERBS WITH "GO"

How are you going to go about fixing this car?

go about
start tackling a problem or task

As soon as I realized Orla had forgotten her bag, I went after her.

go after
follow or chase someone

James went over the company's accounts to check for mistakes.

go over
review

My daughter goes to ballet classes every Saturday morning.

go to
regularly attend

After I got back from the dentist, it took a couple of hours for the pain to go away.

go away
disappear

Michelle and I go back years. I've known her since kindergarten.

go back
know someone for a long time

Buying water in plastic bottles goes against my principles.

go against
be the opposite of what you wish or believe

The children watched the hot-air balloon slowly go up into the air.

go up
move from a lower position to a higher one

A team of firefighters went into the burning building.

go in(to)
enter a building, room, or enclosed space

As soon as the teacher had gone out of the room, the children began misbehaving.

go out (of)
leave a room, building, or enclosed space

See also:
go ahead **56** go around **32** go away **56** go back **16**, **35** go by **15**
go down **12**, **32** go for **47** go out **3**, **5**, **27** go through **19**

Help yourself to some cakes. There are enough to go around.

go around
be enough for everyone

Malachai went through a period of unhappiness after his dog died.

go through
experience something

There's something going on next door. I can hear loud music.

go on
happen

Parents often have to go without sleep when they have a new baby.

go without
live without something

Cath couldn't find the recipe, so she had to make it up as she went along.

go along
continue to do something

My new trainer is called Zachariah, though he usually goes by Zac.

go by
be called by a certain name

Kelly's decided to go for the job at the software company. It's very well paid.

go for
try to achieve something

All the money we make today will go toward funding the new school library.

go toward
contribute to

Rob and I sat on the beach watching the sun go down.

go down
move from a higher position to a lower one

Even though it was a cloudy day, Ramon decided to go ahead with the picnic.

go ahead (with)
decide to do something (after consideration or official approval)

54.2 MATCH UP THE PAIRS OF SENTENCES THAT MEAN THE SAME THING

As soon as the teacher had gone out of the room, the children began misbehaving. → As soon as the teacher had left the room, the children began misbehaving.

1. My daughter goes to ballet classes every Saturday morning.
2. There's something going on next door. I can hear loud music.
3. James went over the company's accounts to check for mistakes.
4. Help yourself to some cakes. There are enough to go around.
5. Malachai went through a period of unhappiness after his dog died.
6. After I got back from the dentist, it took a couple of hours for the pain to go away.

- After I got back from the dentist, it took a couple of hours for the pain to disappear.
- As soon as the teacher had left the room, the children began misbehaving.
- Help yourself to some cakes. There are enough for everyone.
- My daughter attends ballet classes every Saturday morning.
- Malachai experienced a period of unhappiness after his dog died.
- James reviewed the company's accounts to check for mistakes.
- There's something happening next door. I can hear loud music.

54.3 LISTEN TO THE AUDIO, THEN NUMBER THE PICTURES IN THE ORDER YOU HEAR THEM

A ☐

B 1

C ☐

D ☐

E ☐

F ☐

G ☐

H ☐

Aa 54.4 MARK THE SENTENCES THAT ARE CORRECT

How are you going to go about fixing this car? ☑
How are you going to go above fixing this car? ☐

1 

Michelle and I go back years. I've known her since kindergarten. ☐
Michelle and I go up years. I've known her since kindergarten. ☐

2 

My new trainer is called Zachariah, though he usually goes by Zac. ☐
My new trainer is called Zachariah, though he usually went by Zac. ☐

3 

Buying water in plastic bottles goes against my principles. ☐
Buying water in plastic bottles going against my principles. ☐

4 

As soon as I realized Orla had forgotten her bag, I went after her. ☐
As soon as I realized Orla had forgotten her bag, I went before her. ☐

5 

The children watched the hot-air balloon slowly went up into the air. ☐
The children watched the hot-air balloon slowly go up into the air. ☐

Aa 54.5 CROSS OUT THE INCORRECT WORDS IN EACH SENTENCE

Cath couldn't find the recipe, so she had to make it up as she went ~~through~~ / ~~on~~ / **along**.

1. Parents often have to **leave** / **go** / **arrive** without sleep when they have a new baby.
2. Help yourself to some cakes. There are enough to go **among** / **over** / **around**.
3. Kelly's decided to go **for** / **on** / **to** the job at the software company. It's very well paid.
4. Rob and I sat on the beach watching the sun **set** / **go** / **back** down.
5. A team of firefighters went **onto** / **down** / **into** the burning building.
6. All the money we make today will go **forward** / **toward** / **into** funding the new school library.
7. Even though it was a cloudy day, Ramon decided to go **about** / **ahead** / **around** with the picnic.

55 "Put," "take," and "give"

55.1 PHRASAL VERBS WITH "PUT"

Liam finished decorating the cake and put it on a stand.

put on
place something onto a surface

The deliveryman put the parcel down before knocking on the door.

put down
place something you have been carrying on the ground or a surface

Angela is upset about her divorce, but she's trying to put it behind her.

put behind
forget about a bad experience

Can you please be quiet? You're putting me off!

put off
distract someone from focusing

The fitness instructor put the class through a tough training program.

put through
make someone experience something

Forecasters have put out a weather warning for heavy rain and strong winds.

put out
broadcast important information

Cassie followed the instructions carefully to put her new wardrobe together.

put together
build, assemble

Scarlett had to put up with busy trains every day on her way to work.

put up with
tolerate something unpleasant

55.3 PHRASAL VERBS WITH "GIVE"

Martha played the violin as a child, but gave it up when she left school.

give up
stop doing something

The café on the high street is giving out free samples of their new cakes.

give out
give something to people for free

See also: give away **51** give up **26** put off **23** put on **6**, **27**, **41** put through **38** take away **25**, **30** take back **10**, **16**, **44** take in **6**, **51** take off **5**, **6**, **9**, **22** take up **15**, **31**

55.2 PHRASAL VERBS WITH "TAKE"

Jim's mother asked him to take his younger brother along to the skate park.

take along (to)

take someone or something with you

Amara took her mother aside to tell her that she was pregnant.

take aside

take someone to a quieter place to tell them something in private

The waste collectors came to take away the bags of trash.

take away

remove something

Denise took a jar down from the shelf to give her dog a biscuit.

take down (from)

get something from a higher place

Seeing the black clouds, Tim went outside to take the washing in.

take in

carry something inside

The police stopped the criminal and took the stolen money off him.

take off

remove something from someone

Eliza has really taken to golf. She never thought she'd like it.

take to

start to like

The elevator took James up to the top floor of the building.

take up (to)

take someone or something to a higher level

My son had been asking for an ice cream all day. I finally gave in and bought him one.

give in

agree to do something after some resistance

Tom's moving to a smaller apartment so he's giving away some of his belongings.

give away

give something to someone for free (rather than selling it)

Aa 55.4 MATCH THE PICTURES TO THE CORRECT SENTENCES

1 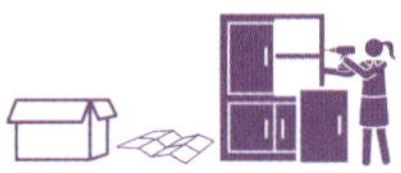

2 

3 

4 

5 

- The police stopped the criminal, and took the stolen money off him.
- The elevator took James up to the top floor of the building.
- Martha played the violin as a child, but gave it up when she left school.
- Cassie followed the instructions carefully to put her new wardrobe together.
- Liam finished decorating the cake and put it on a stand.
- The waste collectors came to take away the bags of trash.

Aa 55.5 CROSS OUT THE INCORRECT WORDS IN EACH SENTENCE

Tom's moving to a smaller apartment so he's giving **away** / ~~**over**~~ / ~~**through**~~ some of his belongings.

1 The café on the high street is **taking** / **putting** / **giving** out samples of their new range of cookies.

2 Denise **got** / **took** / **put** a jar down from the shelf to give her dog a biscuit.

3 Angela is upset about her divorce, but she's trying to **put** / **take** / **give** it behind her.

4 Seeing the black clouds, Tim went outside to take the washing **on** / **off** / **in**.

5 My son had been asking for an ice cream all day. I finally **took** / **gave** / **put** in and bought him one.

Aa 55.6 MATCH THE BEGINNINGS OF THE SENTENCES TO THE CORRECT ENDINGS

	The deliveryman put the parcel	out free samples of their new cakes.
1	The fitness instructor put the class	busy trains every day on her way to work.
2	Scarlett had to put up with	down before knocking on the door.
3	Angela is upset about her divorce,	to tell her that she was pregnant.
4	Amara took her mother aside	She never thought she'd like it.
5	The café on the high street is giving	his younger brother along to the skate park.
6	Eliza has really taken to golf.	but she's trying to put it behind her.
7	Jim's mother asked him to take	through a tough training program.

55.7 LISTEN TO THE AUDIO AND WRITE THE SENTENCES BELOW THE IMAGES

Can you please be quiet? You're putting me off!

1 ______________________

2 ______________________

3 ______________________

4 ______________________

5 ______________________

56 Exclamations

See also:
come in **4** come on **27**, **52** get out **9**, **53**
go ahead **54** go away **54**

56.1 EXCLAMATIONS

Go away!

go away
tell someone or something to leave you alone

Come on!

come on
tell someone or something to follow you or to move faster

Get out!

get out
tell someone to leave a room in an angry way

Look out!

look out
warn someone about something they haven't noticed yet

Are you ready to start?

Yes, bring it on!

bring it on
said when you're confident and ready to start doing something

Hey Vi, can I ask you something?

Sure, fire away.

fire away
let someone know it is fine for them to start talking

I think I've just won the lottery!

Come off it!

come off it
said to express disbelief at something someone has said

Hi Carolina! Come in.

come in
said when inviting someone into a room or building (especially your own home)

Do you mind if I sit here?

Go ahead.

go ahead
said when giving someone permission to do something

56.2 LISTEN TO THE AUDIO AND MATCH THE IMAGES TO THE CORRECT PHRASAL VERBS

1 

2 

3 

4 

come in

get out

fire away

go ahead

bring it on

56.3 WRITE THE CORRECT PHRASAL VERB NEXT TO ITS DEFINITION

said to express disbelief at something someone has said = *come off it*

1. tell someone or something to leave you alone = ____________
2. warn someone about something they haven't noticed yet = ____________
3. said when giving someone permission to do something = ____________
4. let someone know it is fine for them to start talking = ____________
5. said when you're confident and ready to start doing something = ____________
6. tell someone to leave a room in an angry way = ____________
7. tell someone or something to follow you or to move faster = ____________
8. said when inviting someone into a room or building = ____________

go ahead — come on — look out — come in — go away — get out — ~~come off it~~ — bring it on — fire away

R Reference

R1 VERBS AND PARTICLES

A single verb can be followed by different particles or prepositions, which can change the meaning of the verb. In each of these sentences, "break" carries a sense of separation or damage, but the particles change the meaning into something different each time.

Maria and Pablo broke up.
Maria and Pablo ended their relationship.

My car broke down.
My car stopped working.

The handle broke off the vase.
The handle separated from the vase.

Ted broke down and started to cry.
Ted became very emotional and started to cry.

A thief broke into my house.
A thief entered my house illegally.

Gustav broke out of prison.
Gustav escaped from prison.

"Break into" and "break out of" have opposite meanings.

R2 COMMON PARTICLES

Phrasal verb particles often bestow a similar meaning or range of meanings no matter which verb they are used with.

PHRASAL VERBS WITH "UP"

The particle "up" often gives a phrasal verb a meaning of upward movement or increase.

UP

Try to pay your bills as soon as they arrive. They can soon **add up**.
accumulate, build up

The monkey **climbed up** the tree with Kazuo's camera.
move toward the top of something

The train left the station slowly before **speeding up**.
go more quickly

Sadie's anger about her boss's rude behavior had been **building up**.
become bigger or stronger

Clive **lifted** his daughter **up** so that she could see the deer.
raise someone or something

PHRASAL VERBS WITH "DOWN"

The particle "down" often gives a phrasal verb a meaning of downward movement, reduction, or action coming to a stop.

DOWN

All of the banks in our town have **closed down**.
close permanently

You should always **slow down** when you drive past a school.
go more slowly

Your essay's too long, Marcel. You need to **cut** it **down** a bit.
reduce in size

Joanna is **winding down** her business to take another job.
gradually bring to an end

Rob and I sat on the beach watching the sun **go down**.
move from a higher position to a lower one

PHRASAL VERBS WITH "IN"

The particle "in" often gives a phrasal verb a meaning of entering or becoming part of something.

IN

In the evening, I often don't get in until after 7pm.
arrive home

Liam dropped in for a cup of coffee and a chat.
visit someone at their home (informal)

The company has started phasing in new computers.
introduce slowly

We forgot to factor in the local competition.
take into consideration

We were all eating our dinner when the dog burst in.
enter a room or building suddenly

PHRASAL VERBS WITH "OUT"

The particle "out" often gives a phrasal verb a meaning of leaving, being released, or being removed.

OUT

The café is giving out samples of their new range of cookies.
give something to many people

My new headphones filter out background noise.
remove or block something

The new phone model came out today.
be released

I'm so glad that they're phasing these old models out.
replace slowly

Fleur and Clare were getting ready to go out for the evening.
go somewhere with someone

PHRASAL VERBS WITH "ON"

The particle "on" often gives a phrasal verb a meaning of continuation or physically being on something.

ON

Did you **leave** the lights **on** when you left the house?
leave turned on

Can you **hang on** a minute while I grab my umbrella?
wait for a short time (informal)

The fitting rooms are over there if you'd like to **try** the dress **on**.
wear an item of clothing to see if it fits

The journey **dragged on** for hours. The kids were so bored!
continue for a long time (negative)

George and Yolanda **got on** the train to Paris.
enter (public transportation)

PHRASAL VERBS WITH "BACK"

The particle "back" often gives a phrasal verb a meaning of returning or doing something again.

BACK

The mugs I bought online are broken. I'm going to **send** them **back**.
return an item to the seller by mail

We **brought** you **back** some local olives. They're delicious!
return with

I lent Jenny $20 yesterday and she **paid** me **back** today.
return the money you have borrowed

I love receiving letters from my dad. I always **write back** immediately.
reply by letter or email

By the time we **got back**, it was already getting dark.
return

R3 COMMON SEPARABLE PHRASAL VERBS

Some phrasal verbs can be separated by the object of the verb (see page 14). In these cases, the verb is first, then the object, then the particle. This separation can often be optional, unless the object of a separable phrasal verb is a pronoun, in which case it must go between the verb and the particle.

PHRASAL VERB	DEFINITION	SAMPLE SENTENCE
bring around	persuade someone to support your idea	Al's speech **brought** many people **around** to her ideas.
call off	cancel an event	Our manager was busy, so she **called** our meeting **off**.
chop up	cut into small pieces	**Chop** the onions **up** and then fry them for 10 minutes.
clean up	make tidy again	Can you help me **clean** the kitchen **up** please?
cross out	draw a line or lines through a word	I **crossed out** the wrong word and wrote the right one.
give away	give something to someone for free	Tom is **giving** some of his furniture **away**.
give up	stop doing something	Martha used to play the violin, but she **gave** it **up**.
hand out	distribute	The teacher **handed** some worksheets **out**.
leave out	exclude, not include	To make this recipe vegetarian, **leave** the meat **out**.
let in	allow to enter	I **let** the cat **in** when it started to rain.
let out	allow to leave	I **let** the cat **out** every morning after I've woken up.
make up	invent a story to explain something	I don't believe Gio's story, I think he **made** it **up**.
miss out	forget to include someone or something	I thought I'd counted everyone, but I **missed** you **out**.
push back	postpone	Claude is unwell, so needs to **push** our meeting **back**.
put back	return an object to its original place	Paul and Sally **put** their furniture **back** in its place.
put in	place inside	Lisa **puts** her rabbit **in** its cage each evening.
put on	place something onto a surface	Liam **put** the cake **on** a stand.
take out	take someone on a date	Phil **took** me **out** to an expensive restaurant.
take out on	behave in a bad way to someone	Stop **taking** it **out on** me. It's not my fault!
throw away	discard, put in the trash	If the chicken smells bad, you should **throw** it **away**.
throw on	put a piece of clothing on quickly	Tom **threw** a jacket **on** and ran for the bus.
try out	try a new product to see what it is like	Marta couldn't wait to **try** her new games console **out**.
turn on	make something start working	If you're bored, **turn** the television **on**.
write down	record information by writing it	I **wrote** a few ideas **down** before starting my essay.

R4 COMMON INSEPARABLE PHRASAL VERBS

Some phrasal verbs cannot be separated (see page 15). Their object always comes after them, even if it is a pronoun.

PHRASAL VERB	DEFINITION	SAMPLE SENTENCE
carry on	continue doing something	The children **carried on** misbehaving.
catch up with	talk to friends who have not talked to recently	I **caught up with** some friends yesterday.
come across	find something by chance	I **came across** some old photographs while cleaning up.
cut back on	reduce the amount of money you spend	The government wants to **cut back on** spending.
deal with	manage or solve a problem	We learned how to **deal with** difficult customers.
get at	imply, try to say something indirectly	Sorry, I'm not sure what you're **getting at**.
get off	exit (public transportation)	Gine **got off** the bus when it arrived at her stop.
get on	enter (public transportation)	George and Yolanda **got on** the train to Paris.
get on with	concentrate on doing something	I need to get on with my homework.
get out of	exit (a car or taxi)	Be careful when you **get out of** the car.
get over	recover, feel well again	It took me a long time to **get over** the last cold I had.
go over	review	Remember to **go over** your answers carefully.
go with	look good with another piece of clothing	Does this scarf **go with** my jacket?
hear from	receive news from	Have you **heard from** your cousins recently?
keep up with	run at the same speed	Slow down! I can't **keep up with** you!
live up to	be as good as people had hoped	The movie really **lived up to** everyone's expectations.
look after	care for, take responsibility for	My mother **looks after** my children when I'm at work.
look for	search for something	Peter is going to **look for** a job when he leaves school.
look forward to	wait for something with excitement	George was **looking forward to** going to the beach.
look up to	admire someone	Lots of young people **look up to** sports stars.
pull through	survive a serious illness or operation	It was a risky operation, but Josh **pulled through**.
run out of	not have any more of something	We've **run out of** food. Let's go to the store.
turn up	be found (usually by accident)	I lost my passport, but I'm sure it'll **turn up** soon.
weigh in on	add your opinion to an ongoing discussion	The professor **weighed in on** the political debate.

R5 COMMON PHRASAL NOUNS

Some nouns are based on phrasal verbs (see page 16). They are often either combined into one word or joined by a hyphen.

PHRASAL NOUN	DEFINITION	SAMPLE SENTENCE
breakdown	when something (e.g. a vehicle) stops working	A **breakdown** on the highway caused heavy traffic.
break-in	the act of entering a building illegally	There's been a **break-in** at the local bank.
breakup	the end of a romantic relationship	After their **breakup**, John and Helen stayed friends.
checkout	the place in a store where you go to pay	Jenny went to the **checkout** to pay for her groceries.
checkup	an evaluation (especially for your health)	Terry went to the dentist for a **checkup**.
cover-up	the act of hiding information from people	A newspaper exposed the company's **cover-up**.
crackdown	the act of strictly enforcing a law	There's been a **crackdown** on littering in the town.
falling-out	an argument or disagreement	Idris and Giovanni had a **falling-out**.
getaway	a vacation	Ellen and Piers went to Mexico for a short **getaway**.
get-together	a social gathering	I'm having a **get-together** for my 30th birthday.
giveaway	an event where free items are distributed	The bakery did a **giveaway** to attract more customers.
go-ahead	permission to do something	My manager gave me the **go-ahead** to leave early.
input	a contribution of information or an opinion	I asked for my teacher's **input** on my essay.
intake	the amount of something that is taken in	You should limit your daily **intake** of sugar.
kickoff	the start of a sport match (e.g. soccer)	Liverpool are playing soccer tonight. **Kickoff**'s at 7pm.
letdown	a disappointment	I thought I'd like that movie, but it was a real **letdown**.
mix-up	when things are mistaken for each other	This isn't what I ordered. There's been a **mix-up**.
outset	the beginning	Harry has worked hard from the **outset**.
printout	a physical copy of an electronic document	Jim gave everyone a **printout** of the presentation.
setback	a hinderance or delay	There were a lot of **setbacks** during the project.
sleepover	when you sleep at someone else's house	Phoebe went for a **sleepover** at Eliza's house.
stopover	a stop somewhere on your way elsewhere	Our flight to Los Angeles had a **stopover** in New York.
takeout (US) / takeaway (UK)	food that you buy and take elsewhere (especially your own home) to eat	I don't want to cook. Let's order some **takeout** instead.
workout	a period of exercise	Dimitri was exhausted after his **workout**.

R6 COMMON PHRASAL ADJECTIVES

Some adjectives are based on phrasal verbs (see page 17). They are often either combined into one word or joined by a hyphen.

PHRASAL ADJECTIVE	DEFINITION	SAMPLE SENTENCE
backup	supporting or alternative	I always make a **backup** copy of all my files.
beaten-up	old and in a bad state	Ken's finally getting rid of his old, **beaten-up** car.
broken-down	(usually about a vehicle) no longer working	A **broken-down** truck caused delays on the highway.
bygone	of the distant past	These old photographs are from a **bygone** era.
drawn-out	lasting a very long time (negative)	Buying a house can be a stressful, **drawn-out** process.
follow-up	following	My doctor and I scheduled a **follow-up** appointment.
getaway	used to escape	The thieves escaped in a **getaway** car.
incoming	arriving	Everyone rushed to prepare for the **incoming** storm.
knockdown	lower than usual or before	Kemal sold some of his jewelry at a **knockdown** price.
leftover	remaining after the rest has been used	There's some **leftover** chicken in the fridge.
made-up	invented, not true	Wayne is always telling his friends **made-up** stories.
off-putting	unattractive, unappealing	I found the violence in the movie very **off-putting**.
ongoing	in progress	There's an **ongoing** investigation into their finances.
outdated	out of date, old-fashioned	I'm replacing my **outdated** computer with a new one.
outgoing	sociable, extroverted	Kerry is a very friendly and **outgoing** person.
outspoken	opinionated, vocal about your opinions	My dad is very **outspoken** about environmental issues.
outstanding	excellent	Chris's professor told him his essay was **outstanding**.
outstretched	stretched out as far as possible	Finn approached me with his arms **outstretched**.
run-down	in a poor condition	Paolo is renovating an old, **run-down** house.
stressed-out	anxious about something	Somrita is **stressed-out** with work at the moment.
tired out	exhausted	Vi is feeling **tired out** after a long day at work.
upcoming	taking place in the near future	The country is preparing for the **upcoming** election.
uplifting	inspiring, cheerful	Jo was feeling sad, so she watched an **uplifting** movie.
worn out	exhausted, extremely tired	Gerry was completely **worn out** after his run.

Answers

01

1.3
1 People left the stadium in large numbers.
2 He has been flattering him for a favor.
3 They think they are better than her.
4 I found the portrait by chance.

1.4
1 Jordan's aunts fuss over him when they visit.
2 I found it hard to fit in with the art class.
3 Nuwa gathered up the plates from the table.
4 Sandra was asking after you at the park.

1.5
1 Some of the older children have been **ganging** up on me and calling me names.
2 Ava lost her passport ages ago It turned **up** when she was cleaning the living room.
3 Adi has got a temper. He **turned** on me the instant I suggested he buy a new suit.
4 Mel lent Dave her lawnmower a month ago, and she finally got it **back** from him.

1.6
1 turn up 2 watch over 3 turn on
4 wear down 5 pack into

1.7
1 Some of the older children have been **ganging up** on me and calling me names.
2 Mel lent Dave her lawnmower a month ago, and she finally **got** it **back** from him.
3 I got my son a puppy. After asking me for months, he finally **wore** me **down**!
4 Hundreds of people **packed into** the town hall to watch the debate.
5 Barney really **looks up to** his grandfather. He loves listening to his stories.

02

2.3
1 I let the cat in when it started to rain.
2 Olly's dog ran away last week while they were at the park.
3 My mother looks after my children while I'm at work.

2.4
1 After a few days, Olly's dog came back all by herself.
2 Jasmine takes after her mother. They're very similar people.
3 I let the cat out every morning after I've woken up.
4 Albert's parents named him after his great-grandfather.
5 After traveling for a few years, Bill settled down and bought a house.
6 Colin lives with his son in a house at the edge of town.

2.5
1 Lisa puts her rabbit **in** its cage each evening before bed.
2 Will and Joe are identical twins. It's almost impossible to tell them **apart**.
3 After traveling for a few years, Bill settled **down** and bought a house next door to his parents.
4 Liam gets **on** very well with his elder sister. They're always laughing together.
5 Fiona's cat doesn't like strangers, but he's warming **to** Dan.
6 Jenny's grown **out** of her old toys, she prefers playing video games now.

2.6
1 Will and Joe are identical twins. It's almost impossible to **tell** them **apart**.
2 Lisa **puts** her rabbit **in** its cage each evening before bed.
3 Jasmine **takes after** her mother. They're very similar people.
4 I **let** the cat **out** every morning after I've woken up.
5 Jenny's **grown out of** her old toys, she prefers playing video games now.

03

3.3
A 3 B 2 C 1 D 5 E 4 F 6

3.4
1 My brother **set me up** with a woman who works at his office.
2 Jack and Ula **really care for** each other. They've been together for 50 years.
3 They started **going out with** each other when they were at school.
4 Misha **stood by Colin** when he decided to quit college.

3.5
1 go off 2 bring together 3 fizzle out
4 set up 5 drift apart 6 finish with
7 care for

3.6
1 My best friends and I have **stuck together** since high school.
2 For our first date, Phil **took** me **out** to an expensive restaurant.
3 Bernadette **confided in** Martha that she was in love with Pavel.
4 Luisa has **finished with** Ben. He's very upset.
5 Ken **stuck by** Cath when her restaurant went bankrupt.

04

4.3
1 show around 2 invite along 3 show out 4 snoop around 5 stay over

4.4
1 He arrived at 6am.
2 They gave me a tour.
3 They brought their kids with them.
4 We'd like you to come to our home.
5 He visited me at my home.

4.5
1 On her way home from the gym, **Miriam stopped off at the supermarket**.
2 My father came into the house **and took off his coat**.
3 Omar told us to come over **any time after 2pm**.
4 After chatting on the doorstep, **Malik invited me in.**
5 We ended up staying over **at Beth and Omar's** house.
6 While everyone was in the garden, **I found Klaus snooping around inside**.

4.6
1 My new neighbors, Kaito and Leiko, **had** me **over** for dinner last night.
2 We chatted for hours, and he suggested I **stick around** for dinner.
3 On our way home from the beach, we **called in** to see Grandma.
4 Omar told us to **come over** any time after 2pm.
5 While you're in town, try to **swing by**. It would be good to see you.

05

5.3
1 Amara let her little sister tag **along** when she went to the ice rink.
2 Ella likes to get **together** with her friends at the ice cream parlor.
3 I hate to tear you **away**, but we're going to miss the last train.
4 Katie asked Lisa if she wanted to come **out** to play.
5 Joe suddenly took **off** without saying where he was going.

5.4
1 Charlie stormed **out of** the store when the manager refused to give him a refund.
2 As I was leaving for the art exhibition, I asked Joe if he wanted to come **along**.
3 Lots of guests were milling **around**, waiting for Raj to make his speech.
4 Vincent and Maya decided to stay **in**. They ordered pizza and watched a movie.
5 We headed **off to** the beach early because we wanted to avoid the crowds.
6 Once a year, my school friends and I go out for a meal together to catch **up**.

5.5
1 shoot off
2 mill around
3 liven up
4 stay out

5.6
1 Nadiya had to **dash off to pick** up the kids from school.
2 The carnival was amazing. **We stayed out until** dawn.
3 Fleur and Clare were getting **ready to go out** for the evening.
4 Our local hotel has a large room that **it hires out for** parties.

06

6.2
1 All the children at the party had dressed up as dinosaurs.
2 Maurice hung up his coat as he walked in.
3 Angelica helped her son to button up his shirt as he got ready for school.
4 I hope this juice stain comes out when I wash my shirt.

6.3
1 Marlon zipped up his leather jacket and walked toward the door.
2 Gemma's shoes go really well with that dress.
3 Arnie's so proud of his new jacket. He's been showing it off to everyone.
4 Zane folded up his clothes and put them in the wardrobe.

6.4
A 3 B 6 C 1 D 4 E 7 F 2 G 5

6.5
1 Mirek **did up** his coat to keep out the icy breeze.
2 Kelly stopped to **tie up** one of her shoe laces.
3 The sun is really strong today, so make sure you **cover up**.
4 Gio's **grown out of** his sweater, so he's going to give it to his little brother.
5 Alex **put on** her prettiest dress to go out for her wedding anniversary.

07

7.3
1 Heavy traffic has had a strong effect on the city's air quality.
2 Old cell phones aren't as good as today's smartphones.
3 Due to her injury, Colleen had to accept the fact that she couldn't play in the match.
4 To get into college, you'll need to get better results than you got last year.

7.4
1 Sanjay got 100% on his exam. He more than **measured up to** his parents' expectations.
2 The new action movie really **lived up to** the crowd's expectations.
3 The discovery of some ancient ruins has **led to** an increase in tourism.
4 The invention of the computer **brought about** the end of the typewriter.
5 The heavy rain **resulted in** floods throughout the city.

08

8.5
1 not wake up when your alarm rings
2 go to bed
3 go to bed later than usual
4 take a lying position
5 do small tasks in a relaxed way
6 make yourself look clean and tidy
7 get out of bed

8.6
1 sleep over 2 sleep in
3 get in 4 get up
5 go off

8.7
1 wake up
2 head off (to)
3 doze off
4 sit down
5 set about

8.8
1 After a short break, Ramone **got on with** cleaning the bathroom.
2 Martina **stayed up late** studying for her exam the following morning.
3 I tried to wake Mia when I saw she had **dozed off at** her desk.
4 Quite a few people **nodded off during** the speech.

09

9.3
1 I got lost driving to your house. I had to pull over and ask for directions.
2 Tanya turned off the main road and drove along the track to the beach.
3 The helicopter took off from the top of the skyscraper.
4 Gina got off the bus when it arrived at her stop.
5 The train left the station slowly, before speeding up as it headed to the coast.

9.4
1 Jen turned **back** when she realized that she had forgotten her phone.
2 I pulled **up** by the train station to let my daughter out.
3 Sally picked her friends **up** outside the movie theater at 9pm.
4 When you reach the castle, turn **onto** the highway and head west.
5 Jamie dropped me **off** at the train station on his way to work.
6 Angelo left his house and got **into** the taxi.
7 Marion didn't notice the motorcycle as she pulled **out of** the junction.

9.5

1 As the movie star **got out of** the limousine, photographers surrounded him.
2 We **pulled in** at a small roadside café, where we could have some breakfast.
3 The plane **touched down** in Dubai at 9pm in the evening.
4 You should always **slow down** when you drive past a school.
5 Clive tried to restart the motorboat's engine after it **cut out** without any warning.

9.6

1 get on 2 slow down 3 break down
4 drive off 5 turn onto

10

10.2

1 The fitting rooms are over there if you'd like to wear the clothes to see if they fit.
2 The mugs I bought online are broken. I'm going to return them to the seller by mail.
3 I bought my new laptop online, and went to collect it from my local store.
4 Before buying a new car, it's worth visiting several stores to compare prices.
5 I went to the market to buy some bread, but all the bread had been sold.

10.3

1 line up 2 stock up (on) 3 cross off
4 sell out (of) 5 snap up

10.4

1 Marta couldn't wait to **try out** her new games console.
2 Kemal **knocked down** the price of jewelry by 15% to attract shoppers to his new store.
3 Luis put the melon in his basket and **checked it off** his shopping list.
4 Aisha decided to **splash out on** clothes for her summer vacation.
5 Ellie used her credit card to **pay for** the scarf.

10.5

1 Aziz had been looking **around** the store for ages, but couldn't find a shirt he liked.
2 Shoppers had already snapped **up** all the bargains at the sale by the time I'd arrived.
3 Once Ellie had found a scarf that she liked, she went to check **out**.
4 Carla didn't like the sweater she'd bought, so she decided to take it **back**.
5 Joshua crossed **off** each item on the shopping list as he found it.

11

11.2

1 Today started off nicely, so we ate our breakfast on the terrace.
2 After days of bad weather, the rain finally started to let up.
3 Chris and Mel had to leave the beach when it started bucketing down.
4 The weather's been awful, but it's finally starting to brighten up.

11.3

1 Minutes after Ben had lit the grill, the sky clouded over.
2 People go ice-skating when the lake freezes over in the winter.
3 The wind's picking up. It's perfect weather for flying a kite.
4 Alice likes to sit on the balcony when the weather cools down in the evening.

11.4

1 As soon as the storm had **blown over,** the hikers left the cave and continued walking.
2 As dark storm clouds **rolled in** from the east, Arthur tried to get home before the rain started.
3 It looks like the weather's **clearing up**. We'll be able to start the game again soon.
4 By the end of May, the weather starts to **warm up** and the tourists start to arrive.
5 Once the storm had **calmed down**, Grace checked her house for damage.

11.5

A 4 B 1 C 7 D 2 E 6 F 3 G 8 H 5

12

12.4

A 5 B 1 C 7 D 4 E 2 F 6 G 3

12.5

1 When Amy zoomed in, she noticed the red car in front of the restaurant.
2 Some criminals hacked into our computer system and stole the new designs.
3 Pete scrolled up to the top of the document to find the company's address.

12.6

1 You should **shut down** your computer at night to save electricity.
2 **Click on** the link at the bottom of the page to see the answers.
3 I **back up** all my photos in case my computer breaks.
4 Always make sure you **log out** of your account after using it.
5 The company has started **phasing in** new computers. They look great!

12.7

1 I **type out** my essays because it's quicker than writing them by hand.
2 I **printed out** a copy of the contract for the clients to sign.
3 Our company hired a technician to **set up** the new printer.
4 You have to **type in** your password to access the website.
5 Amy **zoomed out** to look at the whole picture at once.

13

13.3

1 One of my old school friends is a candidate for mayor.
2 The police stopped people from entering the area where the crime had taken place.
3 After robbing the store, the thieves escaped in a stolen car.
4 Be aware of pickpockets when you're on the train!
5 The police are becoming stricter on illegal parking in the city.
6 Activists are asking the government publicly to protect the country's forests.

13.4

A 7 B 1 C 4 D 2 E 6 F 3 G 5 H 8

13.5

1 The police ordered the criminal to hand over the stolen money.
2 Senators voted on the new law after a long debate.
3 Janice is leading a campaign to stamp out littering in the park.
4 While I was driving home, the traffic police pulled me over for speeding.
5 Dan tipped off the police about the location of the stolen artworks.

13.6

1 vote for 2 turn to 3 track down
4 beat up 5 bring in 6 call for

14

14.2
1. The company reduced in value.
2. Tommy had to spend a lot of money.
3. I inherited a lot of money.
4. Patrick put money into a bank
5. We paid Wayne what we owed him.

14.3
1. pay up 2. wipe off 3. run up
4. chip in 5. live on
6. save up

14.4
1. Sara has finally **coughed up** the money I lent her last year.
2. I've decided to **cut back on** spending by bringing my own lunch to work.
3. The food was excellent, but we were shocked when the bill **came to** more than $200.
4. The cost of the new stadium has already **run into** the millions.
5. Try to pay your bills as soon as they arrive. They can soon **add up**.

14.5
1. The cost of the new stadium has already run into the millions.
2. The food was excellent, but we were shocked when the bill came to more than $200.
3. Tara and Ali are saving up for a new house. They try to save $300 each month.
4. Tommy had to fork out more than $600 to get his car repaired.
5. Pete went to the ATM to take out some cash.

15

15.3
1. Move more quickly, Oliver.
2. I have more time for my studies.
3. I began to love Phil.
4. He makes lectures last longer.
5. I like to pass the time by reading.
6. He had no more time.
7. Your session has ended due to inactivity.

15.4
1. drag out 2. hurry up 3. wait for
4. break up 5. while away

15.5
1. The journey **dragged on** for hours. The kids were so bored.
2. Commuting to and from work really **eats into** my time.
3. Cleaning the house **took up** all of Liam's weekend.
4. The deadline for the project **crept up on** us.

15.6
1. The service here is terrible! It's **holding everyone up**.
2. Time's **getting on now**. Let's hurry home before it gets dark.
3. Can you **hang on a** minute while I grab my umbrella?
4. The doctor's busy today, but I'll try to **fit you in** tomorrow.

16

16.4
A 6 B 1 C 4 D 2 E 7 F 5 G 3 H 8

16.5
1. In my country, the clocks go **forward** by one hour in the spring.
2. The clocks go **back** by one hour in the fall.
3. Elly and George are looking **forward to** going to the beach later.
4. Claude is unwell today We'll have to push our meeting back **to** tomorrow.
5. Finding my old toys brought **back** happy memories of my childhood.
6. The building project has just begun Months of construction work lie **ahead**.
7. We are planning to turn the store back **into** a house and live there.
8. All the streets were decorated in the weeks leading **up** to the festival.

16.6
1. This dress takes me back to **my childhood in the 1960s**.
2. Kira had dreamed of becoming a great actor, **but her plans didn't pan out**.
3. Peter reminds me of you **when you were a little boy**.
4. Many of the buildings in my city **date back to the 19th century**.
5. The house was turned into **a convenience store in the 1980s**.

16.7
1. The doctor's off tomorrow, so could we **bring** your appointment **forward to** today?
2. Colin is working hard because the deadline for his article is **coming up**.
3. Roland **looks back on** his college days with pleasure.
4. All the streets were decorated in the weeks **leading up to** the festival.
5. I like to listen to music and **think back to** my days as a musician in Paris.
6. The building project has just begun. Months of construction work **lie ahead**.

17

17.3
1. Take traffic delays into consideration when estimating how long the journey will take.
2. We've been meaning to get a new kitchen for years, but haven't found the time for it.
3. Giovanni forgot about the art project, but he managed to do it without preparation.
4. The two directors had several meetings to make the new contract more definite.
5. I asked Sabrina if she wanted to go camping, but she rejected the idea.
6. The negotiating teams stayed up to discuss and reach an agreement on a new treaty.

17.4
1. They stayed up until after midnight **hammering out** a new treaty.
2. Cleo pretended to be sick to **get out of** going out.
3. Dexter was going to ask Becky out, but he **chickened out**.
4. You need to **think ahead** and save money for the future.

17.5
1. You should **plan ahead** before setting off on a long car journey.
2. Seb said he'd help me paint the house, but he **went back on** his promise.
3. **Look ahead** and picture what you want to be doing in five years' time.
4. The store **weaseled out of** giving us a refund by claiming we had broken the vase.
5. Ed had promised to do a bungee jump with me, but **backed out** at the last minute.

17.6
A 6 B 5 C 1 D 3 E 2 F 7 G 4

18

18.4

1. The soup has a tomato and basil flavor.
2. Marcus used his telescope.
3. Robert searched for his glasses.
4. Please listen to me!

18.5

1. stink out
2. look at
3. listen out for
4. listen in on
5. sniff around
6. look through

18.6

1. sniff around 2. look at 3. look out over
4. look away

18.7

1. listen in (on)
2. stink out
3. look out for
4. hear about
5. listen up
6. hear out
7. look on

18.8

1. Alex's cookies **smelled of** cinnamon. I asked to try one.
2. Have you **heard about** the new gym in town? It's supposed to be great.
3. Dayita **listened to** the radio while she ate her breakfast.
4. Fiona **spied on** her colleagues to steal their ideas.
5. Sarah and Dionne **looked into** the well. There was no sign of the bottom.

19

19.3

A 2 B 5 C 1 D 3 E 4

19.4

1. Kazuo got the monkey to climb down **by offering it a banana**.
2. The explorers walked **into the cave**.
3. Doug dropped back to help one of **the other hikers, who had injured himself**.
4. As we came down from the summit, **the weather became much worse**.
5. The saleswoman came up **to Fabio and asked if he needed any help**.
6. Clive lifted his daughter up s**o that she could see the deer**.

19.5

1. When I heard someone calling my name, I turned **around**.
2. Martin was exhausted, and began to **fall** behind the other runners.
3. Clive lifted his daughter **up** so that she could see the deer.
4. Janine grabbed her coat and walked **out** of the room.
5. Doug dropped **back** to help one of the other hikers, who had injured himself.

19.6

1. Tanya **turned away as** the nurse gave her the injection.
2. The monkey **climbed up the** tree with Kazuo's camera.
3. Helen told her son to **get down from** the garden wall.
4. As the train **went through the** mountain range, Ted took some photographs.

20

20.3

1. Leo is the youngest in his class, but manages to keep up with his classmates.
2. She's looking into how astronauts might travel to Mars one day.
3. Sam has dived into his new project. He spent all weekend working on it.
4. The library was full of students swotting up on English grammar.
5. At the start of your presentation, lay out the main points you are going to discuss.

20.4

1. Noah **is majoring in** international politics at college.
2. I kept making mistakes, so I decided **to start over**.
3. Patsy's research **focuses on space** travel.
4. Fiona **worked through the** problems in her code to fix the issues.

20.5

1. work through
2. move on to
3. count toward
4. mark down
5. focus on
6. lay out

20.6

A 5 B 1 C 8 D 3 E 4 F 2 G 7 H 6

21

21.3

1. Schools close in July.
2. Marco did not punish Gio and Carmen.
3. Zosia reprimanded the children.
4. Rosie responds rudely to her teachers.

21.4

1. After the class, Arun packed up his things and got ready to leave.
2. Miguel handed in his assignment just before the deadline.
3. Ramu's working on a huge painting of New York.
4. The teacher handed out the worksheet to each student.

21.5

1. not stand for 2. hand in 3. drop out
4. play up

21.6

1. hand out (to) 2. wipe off 3. not stand for
4. drop out 5. turn to

21.7

1. Good morning class. Please **take out** your books.
2. The kids have been **playing up** all morning.
3. Despite the teacher's warnings, the children **carried on** misbehaving.
4. You've spent too much time **goofing off** this semester, Jesse.
5. Mateo and Juanita are very naughty, but Martina lets them **get away with** it.

22

22.4

1. Ted used to be very proactive, but he's been **slacking off** lately.
2. I've got lots to do! I need to **knuckle down** and get it finished.
3. Angela **meets up with** her colleagues once a week to discuss all their new ideas.

4 Our manager was busy, so she had to **call off** our meeting.
5 Jennie's been **slogging away** trying to finish writing her presentation.
6 Kamal's manager **chased up** the report, which was already a week late.
7 I **clock in** at 9am every morning.

22.5
A, C, D, F, G, I

22.6
1 I'm not feeling very well today, so I'm going to call in sick.
2 I've been very busy lately, but I have next week off work.
3 I clock off at 5pm every afternoon.
4 Ola is carrying out a survey about worker satisfaction.

22.7
1 The applications for the new manager position are **piling up**. I'd better start looking through them.
2 Fiona was struggling to finalize the company's accounts, but she kept **plugging away** at them.
3 Debbie **took** the afternoon **off** so she could go to the dentist.
4 Despite the storm, the engineers **soldiered on** and installed the new phone line.

23

23.2
1 go back to
2 draw on
3 head up
4 stick with

23.3
1 Elliot found the job easily.
2 Katie makes use of her experience.
3 Naina is planning to become a teacher.
4 I went back to work.
5 Diana leads the new department.
6 Chad is looking for jobs in the media.
7 Olivia is trying to become a journalist.

23.4
1 stick with
2 apply for
3 take over
4 go back to
5 wind down

23.5
1 get into
2 burn out
3 branch out (into)
4 put off
5 cash in on
6 fall back on
7 set out

24

24.2
1 The bank agreed to write off the debt, saving Ethan's company from bankruptcy.
2 We are proud to announce that our two banks are entering into a partnership.
3 Mario's gas station has just gone under. It had been struggling for a long time.
4 Katie's trying to drum up interest in her café by offering free samples of her cakes.

24.3
1 Marco's garden center is doing well. It turns **over** almost $250,000 a year.
2 We need the CEO to **sign** off on this important decision.
3 The board has finally **come** to a decision about the new logo for the company.
4 Ellie's company deals **in** antiques. She sells pieces from all over the world.
5 Could you **draw** up a contract for our new clients?
6 The company is facing difficulties. We may need to lay **off** some staff.

24.4
1 fall through
2 come to
3 sign off
4 drum up
5 enter into
6 profit from

24.5
1 Our business is growing, so we are **taking on** more staff.
2 A new bookstore is **opening up** in our neighborhood.
3 Chrissie has just **started up** her own hair salon. It opened last week.
4 Gemma has **bought out** all the other partners.
5 Al's store is **selling off** a lot of its stock.
6 Alan's sportswear company **profited from** the cold weather.

25

25.3
1 The number of people buying clothes online shot up last year.
2 The coach divided the children up into two equal teams.
3 Shreya counted up the number of people wanting coffee and went to make some.
4 When Georgia was paying her check, she added on a 20% tip.

25.4
A 3 B 1 C 6 D 2 E 4 F 5

25.5
1 Katie's bills have been **stacking up**. She's in a lot of debt now.
2 The company's share price has been falling, but it's finally starting to **bottom out**.
3 The temperature varies a bit in the summer, but it **averages out at** about 25°C.
4 We estimated the cost of the project to be £14,900, but **rounded** it **up to** the nearest thousand.
5 If you want to set yourself a budget, start by **adding up** all your monthly expenses.

25.6
1 count down 2 add up 3 average out (at) 4 level out 5 count out 6 bottom out

26

26.4
1 scrape by 2 carry off 3 win out
4 sail through 5 run into 6 give up
7 screw up

26.5
1 screw up 2 carry off 3 win out
4 come off 5 run into

26.6
1 My teachers told me I'd never amount to anything, but now I'm a lawyer.
2 Anita's hard work has paid off. The dress looks beautiful.
3 Many smaller stores have lost out since the supermarket opened in town.
4 Nia built on her experience working at a hotel to set up her own guesthouse.
5 Having supportive parents really contributed to my success.

26.7

1 Clive **muddled through** the interview without any preparation. He was shocked when he got the job.
2 When I didn't get into college, I started my own successful business. Everything **worked out** in the end!
3 The Scottish team **pulled off** an amazing victory, scoring two goals in the last four minutes.
4 When Al saw how many people were making money by selling things online, he decided to **get in on** it.
5 Kwase **sailed through** his driving test. He didn't make any mistakes.

27

27.4

1 If you're bored, **turn on** the television. There's a good movie on tonight.
2 When Ben got home, he realized that he'd forgotten his keys and was **locked out**.
3 My parents have decided to **move away** and live in the country.
4 When Elsa heard her favorite song on the radio, she **turned up** the volume.
5 The street lights **come on** at dusk, when the sun sets.
6 The lights in the house **went out**, so Clara lit some candles.
7 We finally sold our house. We're **moving out** today.

27.5

1 go off
2 move in
3 lock out
4 turn on
5 turn down

27.6

A 3 B 1 C 6 D 2 E 5 F 4

27.7

1 turn off 2 lock in 3 leave on
4 turn down 5 come on

28

28.3

1 put back 2 chop down 3 pitch in
4 pull up 5 take out 6 clear out
7 wash up

28.4

1 Nousha's room looked much nicer after she'd put **up** some pictures.
2 Paul spent the whole afternoon pulling **up** weeds.
3 Karl swept **up** the trash from the party and put it into bags.
4 After finishing the gardening, Scott put his tools **away**.
5 Jason told me to mop **up** the water that I'd spilled on the floor.

28.5

1 The tree in our backyard died, so we had to **chop it down**.
2 I'm **digging up** the lavender bushes so I can move them to a different part of the garden.
3 I **wipe down** the table each evening after we've eaten.
4 We need to **tidy up** before the guests arrive.
5 The hedge in Doug's yard was getting too big, so he **cut it back**.

28.6

1 On Tuesday mornings, I **take** the trash **out**.
2 If the chicken smells bad, **throw** it **out**.
3 Ian **hung** his washing **out** to dry.
4 We **cleared out** the garage this weekend.
5 There was a mess to **clean up** after the party.

29

29.3

1 I always **cut off** the fat from the meat before cooking it.
2 My breakfast typically **consists of** bread and cheese, served with coffee.
3 Nadiya left the cherry pie on the windowsill to **cool down**.
4 Before serving the curry I made sure to **fish out** any bones.
5 My sister can **whip up** a tasty meal in minutes from just a few ingredients.

29.4

1 chop up
2 set aside
3 cut off
4 mix in
5 pour in
6 finish off
7 fish out
8 cool down
9 leave out

29.5

1 Patrick broke up the chocolate before adding it to the cake mixture.
2 My sister can whip up a tasty meal in minutes from just a few ingredients.
3 The sauce boiled over, leaving a mess on the stove top.
4 I always measure out all of my ingredients before trying a new recipe.
5 We managed to fill up three jars with the cookies we'd baked.

29.6

1 After chopping the vegetables, **set** them **aside**.
2 **Cut off** the fat from the meat before cooking it.
3 When the meat is cooked, **pour in** the stock.
4 **Mix in** the eggs with the other ingredients.
5 **Finish off** the stew by adding chopped parsley.
6 Before serving, make sure to **fish out** any bones.
7 For a vegetarian version, **leave out** the meat.

30

30.3

1 I washed down my pizza **with a cold drink.**
2 Our restaurant can cater for **about 100 customers at a time.**
3 After the wedding, **we all drank to the bride and groom.**
4 Lisa shared out the chocolates, **giving the children two each.**
5 I was going to make a lasagna, **but we've run out of pasta.**

30.4

1 Paul and Sarah ordered two hamburgers and sodas to take **away**.
2 The café was about to close, so we drank **up** and got ready to leave.
3 I washed **down** my pizza with a cold drink.
4 After a long day at the beach, my kids wolfed **down** their dinner.
5 Daniel broke **off** a piece of bread and dipped it in the olive oil.

30.5

1 run out of 2 go off 3 eat up
4 wash down 5 go together

30.6

1 eat out 2 top up 3 drink to 4 eat in
5 go together

31

31.3

1 Ken's currently working **toward** getting a black belt in judo.
2 Nathan told his daughters to stop lazing **about**, and help to tidy the house.
3 After the exam, the students went to the local park to wind **down**.
4 I recently got back **into** cycling. I hadn't done it since I was a teenager.
5 On Friday evenings, Josh likes to kick **back** and watch some television.
6 Anastasia absolutely lives **for** skiing. She goes to the mountains whenever she can.

31.4

1 Adi's painting skills are really coming along. He might become an artist one day.
2 I found running very hard when I started, but I get a lot of satisfaction out of it now.
3 Learning the piano isn't easy, but if you stick at it, you could become a great pianist.
4 Fabio could have been a great guitarist, but he threw it all away by never practicing.

31.5

1 curl up 2 start out 3 sit around
4 live for

31.6

1 I spend most Sundays lying about the house.
2 Aden needs to loosen up and dance with us.
3 On my days off, I like to sit around the garden.
4 Luiza spent the evening curled up on the couch.
5 After a stressful day, I take a bath to chill out.

32

32.2

1 heal up 2 throw up 3 flare up
4 come around 5 seize up 6 go around

32.3

1 Elaine's rash began to clear **up** after she started using the cream.
2 I think I'm coming down **with** the flu.
3 Ella's been throwing **up** all day.
4 My son passed **on** the virus to his sisters.
5 It's taken me weeks to get **over** this cold, but I finally feel better.

32.4

1 Paola's hay fever usually **flares up** in the spring.
2 After a few hours, the swelling had started to **go down**.
3 Danny's thumb **swelled up** after he was stung by a wasp.
4 My brother's a nurse. He **cares for** sick people at the local hospital.
5 I was very sad to hear that your grandmother has **passed away**.

32.5

1 care for 2 feel up to 3 go around
4 wear off 5 pull through

33

33.3

1 After finishing the race, Sandra warmed **down** by stretching her legs.
2 Jamal was completely wiped **out** after cycling up the mountain.
3 Clara was sent **off** the pitch after pushing over another player.
4 Five runners have gotten **through** to the final. Whoever wins this race will win the trophy.
5 My sister is a judo champion She ranks **among** the best in the country.
6 I struggle to keep **up** with my brother. He's much fitter than I am.

33.4

1 Before playing a game of soccer, I always warm up by jogging slowly.
2 For this yoga position, you have to stretch your arms out as far as you can.
3 Pete wanted to start playing baseball, so he signed up for his school team.
4 Angela knocked Kirsten out in the first round of the competition.
5 My knee injury kept me from completing the marathon this year.

33.5

1 Clara was sent off the pitch after pushing over another player.
2 The crowd cheered Tony on as he approached the finish line.
3 I picked up my bow and aimed another arrow at the target.
4 Playing tennis all afternoon with Gus has worn Charlie out.
5 Leo works out at his local gym every morning.

33.6

1 keep up (with) 2 warm up 3 size up
4 turn around 5 burn off 6 cheer on
7 work off

34

34.4

1 The new music channel is **aimed at** people who like jazz.
2 At the start of the horror movie, scary music started to **fade in**.
3 My new headphones help me concentrate by **filtering out** background noise.
4 This new TV show **feeds on** people's curiosity about aliens.
5 The noise from the parade **faded away** as it moved away from us.
6 I **tune into** my favorite radio show every Sunday morning.

34.5

1 This new TV show feeds on people's curiosity about aliens.
2 I tune into my favorite radio show every Sunday morning.
3 The architects have mocked up a model of the new museum.
4 The new music channel is aimed at people who like jazz.
5 Greg and Chloe colored in pictures of dinosaurs after their trip to the museum.

35

35.2

1 get around
2 check in
3 get back from
4 put up
5 soak up

35.3

1 We brought you back some local olives.
2 They checked out of the hotel.
3 Marimar and I went off to Miami recently.
4 It was great to get away for a few days!

35.4

1 On our way to Barcelona, **we stopped over in a hotel for the night**.
2 Whenever we set out on a hike, **we always take a compass and a map**.

3 We set off for Chicago at dawn **when there would be less traffic**.
4 When she arrived at the hotel, **Julia went to the reception to check in**.
5 We managed to put the tent up **even though it was raining heavily**.

35.5

1 When Krishna **arrived at** the villa, the party had begun.
2 We're **packing in** lots of sightseeing during our vacation.
3 It was great to **get away** for a few days.
4 We've been in Cyprus for a few days, but we're **heading for** Athens on today.
5 On your way to London, you'll **pass by** Cambridge.

36

36.2

1 Kirsty talked the workers **through the new software system**.
2 Shona wanted to dye her hair purple, **but her sister talked her out of it**.
3 Diana is always rambling on about **how things were better when she was a child**.
4 Uncle Toby still talks down to me **like I'm a child, even though I'm 25**.
5 Shut up **and listen to me for once!**
6 My kids talked me into **getting a puppy**.

36.3

1 drown out
2 mouth off
3 ramble on
4 tone down
5 talk down
6 launch into

36.4

A 6 B 1 C 2
D 4 E 3
F 5

36.5

1 I think you should **tone down** your language.
2 Andy **blurted out** the name of the winner by mistake.
3 The lecturer **droned on** for what felt like hours.
4 Marco is always **talking at** people and not letting them speak.
5 After the concert, I **struck up** a conversation with the guitarist.

36.6

1 Ben's not keen on buying a new car. I'm trying to **talk** him **round**.
2 When soccer **came up in** conversation, Bill and I realized we support the same team.
3 Craig was trying to tell a joke, but **tailed off** as he realized that no one was listening.
4 While Julia was explaining her idea, Rupert **cut in** to tell her she was wrong.
5 Simone spent the whole of lunch **mouthing off** about how much she hates her new boss.

37

37.3

1 make written notes
2 reduce in size
3 write or type something in full from notes
4 write something quickly or roughly
5 represent, be an abbreviation for
6 read with great attention
7 complete a form

37.4

1 Before you can use the gym, you need to fill in this form.
2 As the judge read out the names of the winners, Pablo waited hopefully.
3 When completing the form, Damian wrote in his age.
4 Alexandra flicked through a magazine while she waited to get her hair cut.

37.5

1 Max **read through** the full report before giving his opinion.
2 Ted always **writes out** his essays instead of typing them.
3 "UFO" **stands for** Unidentified Flying Object.
4 The journalist **jotted down** the details as Dan described his role in the new movie.
5 Fatima **read up** on ancient Greece before her history exam.

37.6

1 I'll try to cut **out** 500 words from my essay if it is too long.
2 *Adventures in the Wilderness* should make **for** interesting reading!
3 Paco read the book and noted **down** the most important points.
4 We **pored over** the old document looking for clues.

38

38.4

1 Rob wants to **follow** up on the conversation we had about the new logo.
2 Claudia sent wedding invitations **out** to all her friends and family.
3 Dave passed **on** a message telling me that Rob had called.
4 Sorry, I can't hear you very well, I'm afraid. You keep **breaking** up.
5 I've called Olly a few times this evening, but I can't get **through**.
6 Could you please speak **up**? I can't hear you very well!

38.5

1 Chris emailed me a week ago, but I only just remembered to email him back.
2 Murat completed all the forms and sent them off to the passport office.
3 I love receiving letters from my dad. I always write back immediately.
4 Claudia sent wedding invitations out to all her friends and family.

38.6

1 put through 2 pick up 3 call back
4 speak up

38.7

1 Anna works from home on Tuesdays, so she will **dial into the** meeting.
2 I'll **put you through** to Mr. Yamamoto now, madam.
3 Our company is trying to **reach out to** new customers by offering discounts.
4 After chatting for over an hour, Simon and I said goodbye **and hung up**.
5 Hi Laura, sorry I'm cooking at the moment, can I **call you back** in 10 minutes?

39

39.4

A 3 B 1 C 7 D 2 E 5 F 4 G 8 H 6

39.5

1 When my husband suggested buying a new kitchen, I did what he suggested.
2 When I told my friends I was starting my own business, they all offered support.
3 They gave us too much information during the training course.

4 Experts believe that Joan Miró created this painting because of the distinctive style.
5 The artist's feelings of anger are communicated strongly in this painting.

39.6
SEPARABLE:
bombard with
bounce off
think over
think through
put to

INSEPARABLE:
run with
come across
touch on
come up with
get behind

39.7
1 The creative manager asked her team to **throw out** as many ideas as they could.
2 It finally **dawned on** me that Claude was the killer.
3 We have **ruled out** three of the candidates. It's a choice between Danny and Carmen.
4 Ted has **come up** with some good ideas for a new logo.
5 Selma is very creative. She **thinks up** lots of wonderful dishes.

40

40.2
1 expand on
2 dumb down
3 come back to
4 point out
5 go back over

40.3
1 put across 2 dumb down
3 point out 4 come back to
5 allude to 6 go back over

41

41.3
1 see through
2 gloss over
3 cover up
4 add up
5 fall for
6 make up
7 level with

41.4
1 make out
2 level with
3 mess around
4 add up
5 put on
6 catch on

41.5
1 I think she knows more than she's **letting on**.
2 We **fell for** the salesman's talk. The car we bought broke down after a few days.
3 When it **came out** that he was bankrupt, I was shocked!
4 Conan finally **owned up** to breaking the window. He'd been denying it all morning.
5 The CEO has been **playing down** the company's financial problems.
6 I've been trying to **find out** from Nisha who Sammy's dating.
7 Josie tried to **explain away** the damage to my car by saying it was just a small scratch.

42

42.2
1 Helen has put me onto this great new hair salon. I'm going to check it out.
2 Lisa's speech in favor of a new nature reserve has brought many people around to the idea.
3 Kendra was very nervous, but was happy to see her friends rooting for her.
4 Zoe's daughter said her elder brother had put her up to stealing the cookies.

42.3
1 Kendra was very nervous, but was happy to see her friends **rooting for** her.
2 Rahul was skeptical about electric cars until the salesman **reasoned with** him.
3 The crowd **urged** Mona **on** as she approached the end of the tightrope.
4 He eventually **won** him **over** by explaining how eco-friendly they are.
5 My son was upset, so I bought him an ice cream to **buck** him **up**.

43

43.3
1 During the debate, she hit out at her opponents.
2 I can count on my sister to comfort me when I'm upset.
3 Paul usually shrugs off criticism of his cooking.
4 Carla stood up to the bullies and told them not to be mean.
5 He pulled her up on her attitude towards the environment.

43.4
B, C, D, F, H, I

43.5
1 Everyone agrees **with** John that Sian should get the job.
2 Everyone criticized Magda's art, but she rose **above** it and is a successful artist now.
3 The workers are pushing **back on** the management's policies.
4 They disagreed **with** each other about what color to paint the kitchen.

43.6
1 My aunt disapproves.
2 Paulina always supports our boss.
3 Laura opposed Ankita's proposals.
4 Carla defended herself.
5 They need to solve small problems.

43.7
1 I think Sonia **has** something **against** me. She never wants to talk to me.
2 Martin and Simon **disagreed with** each other about what color to paint the kitchen.
3 Our local representative has **come out against** the plans for a new housing development.
4 Donna bought her brother some chocolates to **make up for** the things she had said to him.
5 Terry's colleagues always make fun of his shirts, but he just **laughs** it **off**.

44

44.4
1 back off 2 speak out 3 take back
4 stay out of 5 patch up 6 base on
7 stick up for

44.5

A 3 B 6 C 1 D 2 E 5 F 4

44.6

1 back off 2 stay out of
3 back up 4 stick up for
5 fall out (with) 6 lash out (at)
7 back down

44.7

1 When Pete showed Martin the facts, Martin had to **climb down** and admit he was wrong.
2 The manager **laid into** the players after they lost another match.
3 They had **fallen out** when they both applied for the same job.
4 Craig's parents finally caved **in** and bought him a games console.
5 Sorry, I'm not sure what you're **getting at**.

45

45.3

1 Ed's become stronger.
2 She has helped me manage my problems.
3 Kathy is trying to recover from it.
4 Anna became happier.

45.4

1 work through
2 crack up
3 settle down
4 light up
5 burst out

45.5

1 Donny's face lit **up** when he saw the presents waiting for him on the table.
2 Jack's a very private person, but he finally opened **up** and told me how he feels.
3 When Linda feels stressed, she listens to music to help her calm **down**.
4 The children burst **out** laughing when the clown pretended to fall over.

45.6

1 I've been **checking up on** Andrei every day since he lost his job.
2 Craig had had a bad day at work, but watching a funny movie **cheered him up**.
3 Hiro's jokes are hilarious. He really **cracks me up**.
4 Yana was upset, but she **brightened up when** I bought her tickets to a concert.

45.7

1 Sophie needs to **lighten up**. She's still studying even though it's her birthday today.
2 I really **feel for** Kim. She's been so upset since her cat went missing.
3 Kathy is finally **moving on** after her breakup with Jamal last year.
4 Petra's been sulking for days. I wish she'd **snap out of** it.

46

46.2

1 My husband tenses up whenever **I try to talk about money with him**.
2 This song is so moving. **It always sets me off**.
3 Troy freaked out when he noticed **the enormous spider climbing up the wall**.
4 Clare flew into a rage when **her computer crashed and lost all her work**.
5 Stop taking it out on me. **It's not my fault the weather is awful**.
6 My grandchildren love to wind me up. **They're always playing tricks on me**.

46.3

1 Sadie's anger about her boss's rude behavior had been **building up**.
2 Tamal and Sam **choked up** when the hero died at the end of the movie.
3 When Lisa walked onto the stage she **froze up**. She couldn't say anything!
4 He eventually **broke down** and admitted that he was really upset.
5 My manager **blew up** when I told him that I'd left my work laptop on the train.

46.4

1 Bella **welled up** when Pete asked her to marry him.
2 It eventually **spilled over**, and Sadie told her how she felt.
3 Chris had been **bottling up** his emotions for a long time.
4 Work has been **weighing on** me a lot recently.
5 Clare **flew into** a rage when her computer crashed and lost all her work.

46.5

1 get down
2 wind up
3 break down
4 blow up

47

47.2

1 Sonia opted **out** of the boat trip. She always gets sea sick.
2 Yasmin has been toying **with** the idea of getting her hair cut short.
3 The workers wanted a 5% pay raise, but settled **for** 3%.
4 Shona regrets her decision to quit, but she's going to have to live **with** it.
5 After a lot of thought, Rob went **for** the fish instead of the steak.

47.3

1 decide on
2 factor in
3 mull over
4 pick out
5 opt out
6 lean toward

47.4

1 weigh up 2 narrow down 3 pick out
4 sleep on 5 lean toward

47.5

1 Moving to New Zealand next year **hinges on us** saving enough money.
2 Can you tell us how you **settled on a** winner?
3 Lisa found it hard to choose a dress, but eventually **decided on the** red one.
4 Stephen is **banking on this** new recipe to impress his guests.

48

48.2

A 3 B 5 C 1 D 4 E 2

48.3

1 I was relying on Selma to bring candles for the cake, but she **let** me **down**.
2 I'll never **live down** the time I dropped Erin's birthday cake in the middle of her party.
3 Coralie's graph didn't make sense, so she looked through the data again to see where she'd **slipped up**.
4 When Chris got home from work, he realized that he had **mixed** his bag **up with** Simon's.
5 The spelling mistake in Juanita's homework **jumped out at** me.

49

49.4

1 After the leak in the room above, it looked like the ceiling might fall in.
2 The dog knocked over the plant pot as it chased the cat.
3 Jorge took the old clock apart to fix it.
4 When I got home, I found that the dog had torn a cushion apart.

49.5

A 3 B 1 C 4 D 6 E 2 F 5

49.6

1 smash up
2 wear out
3 bang into
4 trip over
5 fall in
6 break off

49.7

1 I **banged into** the door while leaving the house.
2 Colin accidentally drove into a tree and **smashed up** his van.
3 Rodrigo slammed the door so hard that the pictures **fell off** the wall.
4 The old book **came apart** in the librarian's hands.
5 The drain was **clogged up** with old leaves, so I had to unblock it.
6 Sanjay's old car is **falling apart**. He's had it since he was a teenager.
7 The old manor house Andrei wants to buy looks as if it's about to **fall down**.

50

50.2

A 5 B 1 C 6 D 4 E 2 F 3 G 8 H 7

50.3

1 Whenever Gitanjali has a problem, she goes to her grandmother for advice.
2 While climbing the mountain, we had to deal with strong winds and heavy rain.
3 The proposals for a new highway have encountered a lot of local opposition.
4 One of the pipes was leaking, so we asked a plumber to fix it.
5 Writing your thesis is easier if you separate it into small sections.
6 It's taken me all evening to find out how to turn on this new television.

50.4

SEPARABLE:
break down
thrash out
brush aside
think through

INSEPARABLE:
turn to
come up against
crop up
get around

50.5

1 turn out 2 think through 3 sort out
4 clear up 5 brush aside 6 thrash out
7 check out

51

51.3

1 I didn't mean to tell the team **that it was your birthday. It just slipped out**.
2 The movie star tried to hush up **the fact that she had a new boyfriend**.
3 Jessica has been keeping **the name of her new boyfriend from me**.
4 I was bowled over when Nadia announced **that she had been accepted into dance school**.
5 Mollie crept up on her grandfather **while he slept in the garden**.

51.4

1 Clara can't believe she passed her exams. It's going to take a while for it to sink **in**.
2 People have woken **up** to the fact that we need to look after the environment.
3 I was shopping at the antiques market when I stumbled **upon** a valuable necklace.
4 My best friend **sprang** it on me last night that she's moving to Canada.
5 I was taken **aback** when Tia and Juan told me they were getting married.

51.5

1 play along 2 bump into 3 cotton onto
4 give away

51.6

1 I stumbled upon a valuable necklace at the antiques market.
2 Jessica has been keeping the name of her new boyfriend from me.
3 Mollie crept up on her grandfather while he slept in the garden.
4 We were all eating our dinner when the dog burst into the room.

52

52.4

1 be removed
2 appear (on screen)
3 do something to solve a problem
4 have an opinion of something
5 go toward a place
6 escape with something
7 abolish, no longer need or use

52.5

A 6 B 5 C 1 D 3 E 2 F 4

52.6

1 Riya was disappointed with her wedding cake, and insisted it be **done over**.
2 With hot weather expected, thousands of tourists **made for** the coast.
3 Lots of talented people **make up** our circus's team of acrobats.
4 Natsuo **came across** the room to speak to us.
5 The council has to decide what it's going to **do about** the litter problem.
6 Luanne struggled to **make out** what the train conductor was saying.
7 No matter how much we clean it, this graffiti won't **come off** the wall.

52.7

1 Hetty's career as a musician **came about** after a producer saw her performing.
2 Derek sat down in front of the TV when the ten o'clock news **came on**.
3 Luanne struggled to **make out** what the train conductor was saying.
4 When I tried to log in, a message **came up** saying that my account had been blocked.
5 Lots of talented people **make up** our circus's team of acrobats.

53

53.3

1 Cheryl's dog keeps **getting over** the fence into the neighbor's backyard.
2 Harry burned the dinner and **set off** the smoke detector.

3 As Martin walked home late at night, fear began to **set in**.
4 It's almost eleven o'clock. We should **get down to** work.
5 Mary **set out** all her qualifications and experience in her resume.
6 Lee's speed **sets him apart from** the other players in the tournament.

53.4
SEPARABLE:
set back
set on
get across
get together

INSEPARABLE:
get around
get up (from)
get to
set in

53.5
1 set on 2 get to 3 set back
4 get back at 5 get across
6 get together 7 set up

53.6
1 Lee **got** his fishing **rod out** of the garage and carried it to his car
2 The security guard threatened to **set** his dog **on** us if we didn't leave immediately
3 Can you help me **get** the shopping **in**, please?
4 Before accusing Simon, the police had to **get** their facts **together**.
5 As soon as we **got to** the ski resort, we went straight to the slopes.

54

54.2
1 My daughter attends ballet classes every Saturday morning.
2 There's something happening next door. I can hear loud music.
3 James reviewed the company's accounts to check for mistakes.
4 Help yourself to some cakes. There are enough for everyone.
5 Malachai experienced a period of unhappiness after his dog died.
6 After I got back from the dentist, it took a couple of hours for the pain to disappear.

54.3
A 5 B 1 C 2 D 6 E 4 F 3
G 8 H 7

54.4
1 Michelle and I go back years. I've known her since kindergarten.
2 My new trainer is called Zachariah, though he usually goes by Zac.
3 Buying water in plastic bottles goes against my principles.
4 As soon as I realized Orla had forgotten her bag, I went after her.
5 The children watched the hot-air balloon slowly go up into the air.

54.5
1 Parents often have to **go** without sleep when they have a new baby.
2 Help yourself to some cakes. There are enough to go **around**.
3 Kelly's decided to go **for** the job at the software company. It's very well paid.
4 Rob and I sat on the beach watching the sun **go** down.
5 A team of firefighters went **into** the burning building.
6 All the money we make today will go **toward** funding the new school library.
7 Even though it was a cloudy day, Ramon decided to go **ahead** with the picnic.

55

55.4
1 Cassie followed the instructions carefully to put her new wardrobe together.
2 The waste collectors came to take away the bags of trash.
3 Martha played the violin as a child, but gave it up when she left school.
4 The police stopped the criminal, and took the stolen money from him.
5 Liam finished decorating the cake and put it on a stand.

55.5
1 The café on the high street is **giving** out samples of their new range of cookies.
2 Denise took a jar **down** from the shelf to give her dog a biscuit.
3 Angela is upset about her divorce, but she's trying to **put** it behind her.
4 Seeing the black clouds, Tim went outside to take the washing **in**.
5 My son had been asking for an ice cream all day. I finally **gave** in and bought him one.

55.6
1 The fitness instructor put the class **through a tough training program**.
2 Scarlett had to put up with **busy trains every day on her way to work**.
3 Angela is upset about her divorce, **but she's trying to put it behind her**.
4 Amara took her mother aside **to tell her that she was pregnant**.
5 The café on the high street is giving **out free samples of their new cakes**.
6 Eliza has really taken to golf. **She never thought she'd like it**.
7 Jim's mother asked him to take **his younger brother along to the skate park**.

55.7
1 Denise took a jar down from the shelf to give her dog a biscuit.
2 Angela is upset about her divorce, but she's trying to put it behind her.
3 Seeing the black clouds, Tim went outside to take the washing in.
4 Eliza has really taken to golf. She never thought she'd like it.
5 Amara took her mother aside to tell her that she was pregnant.

56

56.2
1 fire away 2 come in 3 bring it on
4 go ahead

56.3
1 go away 2 look out 3 go ahead
4 fire away 5 bring it on 6 get out
7 come on 8 come in

Index of phrasal verbs

Numbers refer to the module number

D

E

F

G

H

I

J

K

L

M

Acknowledgments

The publisher would like to thank:
Ankita Awasthi Tröger and Hina Jain for editorial assistance; Anna Scully and Noopur Dalal for design assistance; Laura Caddell for proofreading; Christine Stroyan for audio recording management; ID Audio for audio recording and production; DTP Designer Harish Aggarwal; Jackets Editorial Coordinator Priyanka Sharma; and Managing Jackets Editor Saloni Singh.